SUN SIGNS

MOON SIGNS

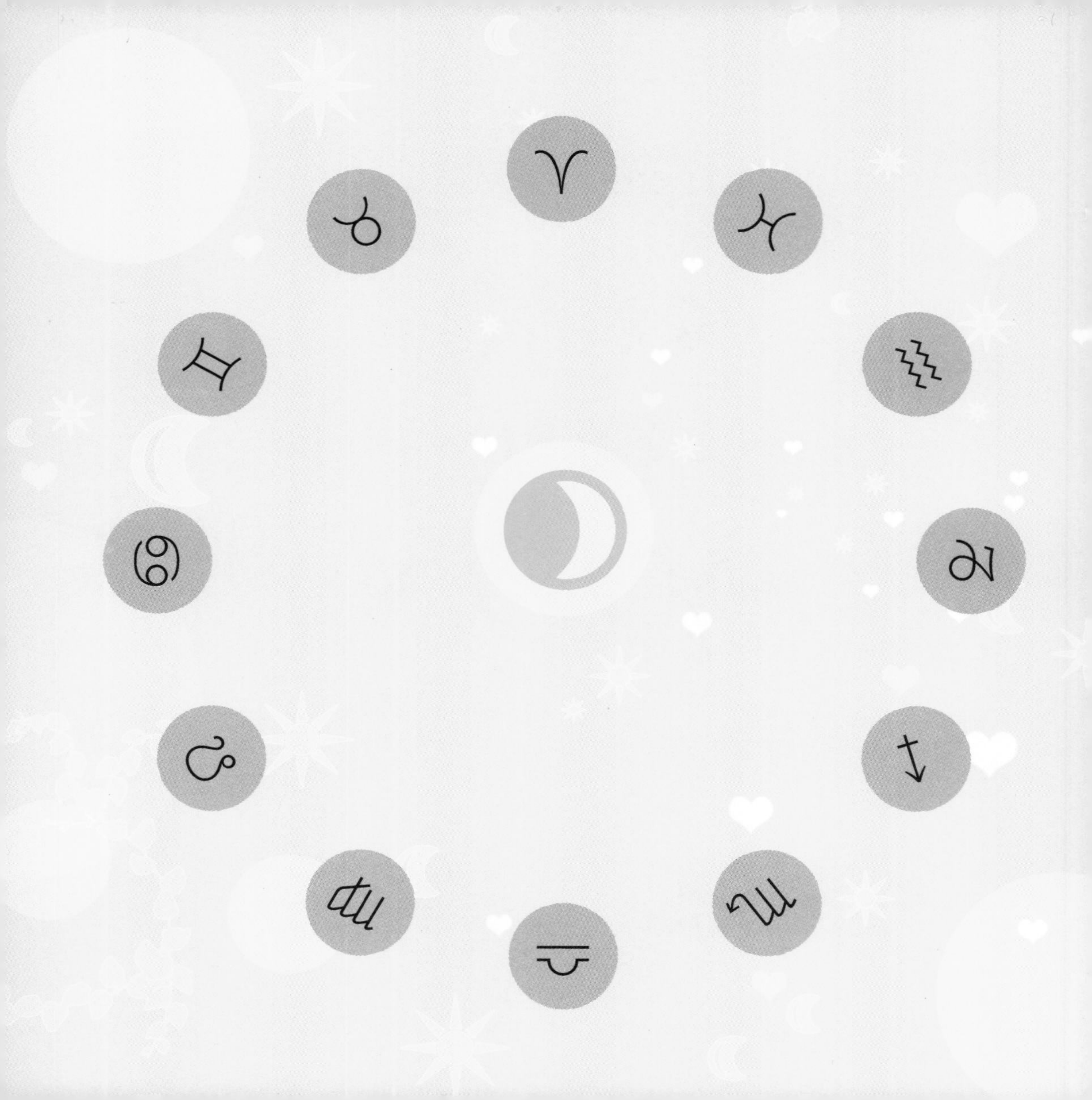

LORI REID

SUN SIGNS

DISCOVER YOUR DESTINY

MOON SIGNS

DUNCAN BAIRD PUBLISHERS
LONDON

To Sophie and Al, my Moon and Sun, who light up my night and day.

Sun Signs/Moon Signs
Lori Reid

Distributed in the USA and Canada by
Sterling Publishing Co., Inc.
387 Park Avenue South
New York, NY 10016-8810

This edition first published in the UK and USA in 2009 by Duncan Baird Publishers Ltd
Sixth Floor, Castle House
75–76 Wells Street
London W1T 3QH

Copyright © Duncan Baird Publishers 2009
Text copyright © Lori Reid 2009
Artwork copyright © Duncan Baird Publishers 2009

The right of Lori Reid to be identified as the Author of this text has been asserted in accordance with the Copyright, Designs and Patents Act of 1988.

All rights reserved. No part of this book may be reproduced in any form or by any electronic or mechanical means, including information storage and retrieval systems, without permission in writing from the publisher, except by a reviewer who may quote brief passages in a review.

Managing Designer: Manisha Patel
Designer: Rachel Cross
Managing Editor: Grace Cheetham
Editor: Judy Barratt
Commissioned artwork: Flatliner V2

Library of Congress Cataloging-in-Publication Data available

ISBN: 978-1-84483-475-4
10 9 8 7 6 5 4 3 2 1

Typeset in Optima
Color reproduction by Colourscan, Singapore
Printed in China by Imago

Author's Acknowledgments

The author would like to thank everyone at DBP for their work on this book, and especially Grace Cheetham, Judy Barratt, Manisha Patel, and Rachel Cross for their editorial sensitivity and immense creative skill. A huge thank you, too, to Jason Jaroslav Cook at V2 for bringing my words alive with his beautiful artwork. May the Sun spark joy in your hearts and the Moon enchant your souls with her mystery and awe.

For information about custom editions, special sales, premium and corporate purchases, please contact Sterling Special Sales Department at 800-805-5489 or specialsales@sterlingpub.com.

Contents

Sun Signs

Introducing the Sun Signs 8
Elemental Sympathies 10

♈ Aries 12
♉ Taurus 16
♊ Gemini 20
♋ Cancer 24
♌ Leo 28
♍ Virgo 32
♎ Libra 36
♏ Scorpio 40
♐ Sagittarius 44
♑ Capricorn 48
♒ Aquarius 52
♓ Pisces 56

Predicting the Future 60
Working with the Wheel of Time 62
Making the Future Work for You 66

Moon Signs

Introducing the Moon Signs 70
How to Find Your Moon Sign 72

♈ Aries Moon 76
♉ Taurus Moon 80
♊ Gemini Moon 84
♋ Cancer Moon 88
♌ Leo Moon 92
♍ Virgo Moon 96
♎ Libra Moon 100
♏ Scorpio Moon 104
♐ Sagittarius Moon 108
♑ Capricorn Moon 112
♒ Aquarius Moon 116
♓ Pisces Moon 120

Timing for Success 124
Making the Most of the Lunar Trends 126

ASTROLOGY OF THE SUN

SUN
SIGNS

Introducing the Sun Signs

Telling someone that you're a Libra, a Virgo or a Sagittarius is simply a shorthand way to describe all sorts of things about you. For a start, your astrological sign tells us what part of the heavens the Sun was in at your time of birth. And because each sign of the Zodiac is associated with a certain group of characteristics, your Sun sign gives an instant snapshot of the kind of person you are.

Just as the spring, with its mild weather and new growth, is different from the winter, with its bitter cold and barren trees, so Taurus is quite different in character from Leo, or Scorpio or Pisces. Essentially, your Sun sign is a mirror in which to see yourself, and through which to learn more about your dreams, hopes and motivations. Your Sun sign reveals how you present yourself to the world, and how you are perceived by others.

It's also worth bearing in mind that Sun signs come in pairs. Your opposite sign is essentially the opposite side of your coin. For example, if you're a Cancer, you may not agree with everything a Capricorn stands for (and vice versa), but you could certainly learn a great deal from each other. So, to round off the picture, take a peek at your opposite sign, too.

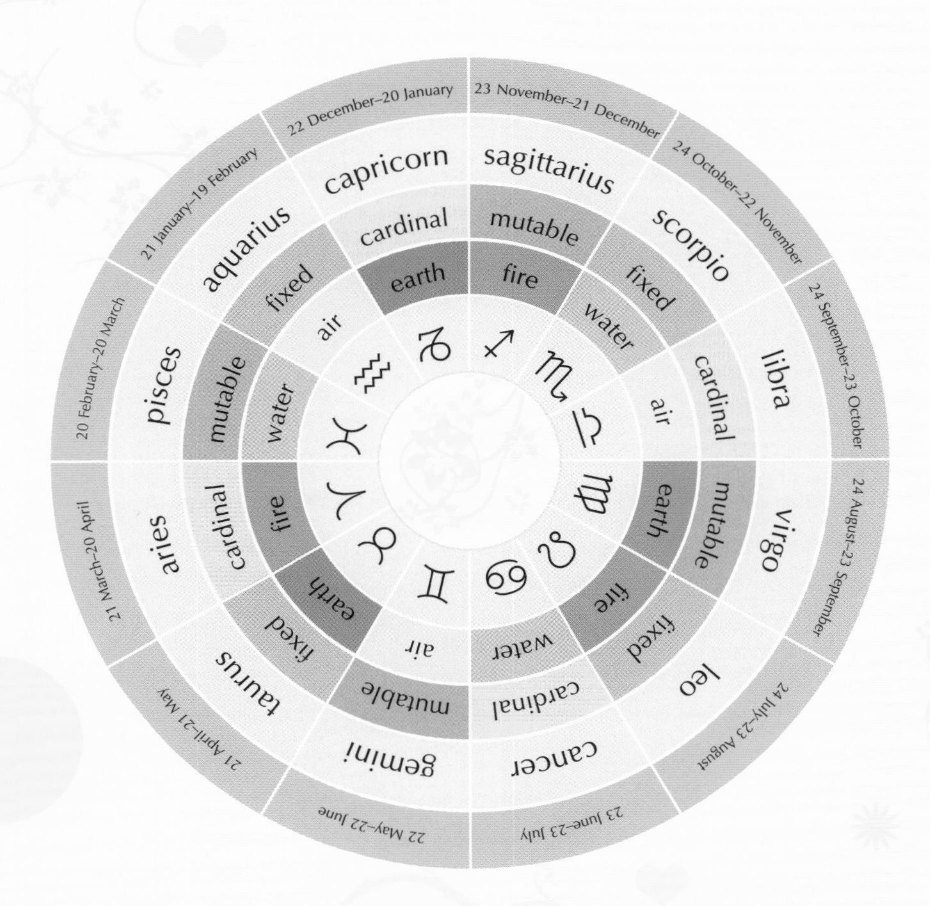

This wheel shows all 12 Sun signs and the times of the year associated with each. Your Sun sign is the sign that covers your birthday. Each sign also has a related Quality and Element (see pages 10–11) and a symbol, known as a glyph.

Elemental Sympathies

Do you feel in tune with your partner, sing from the same song sheet as your boss, share similar interests with your sister, or find you can discuss your deepest feelings with a particular friend? If you do, it's probably because you belong to the same Element "family". People born within the same Element group of signs tend to experience the world in similar ways and so are more likely to get along with each other; they tend to be temperamentally alike and to express themselves similarly, making communication easy and harmonious.

In Western astrology, there are four Elements – Earth, Air, Fire and Water. The table at the top of the opposite page shows which Sun signs belong to which Elements, and how the Elements influence their members' temperaments.

As well as the Elements, certain signs deal with circumstances in corresponding ways. These specific approaches to situations group the signs into what are known as three distinct Qualities: Cardinal, Fixed and Mutable. The bottom table (opposite) shows which Sun signs belong to which Quality, and how each Quality group approaches situations to get things done.

The Element groups

EARTH **Signs:** ♉ ♍ ♑ **Temperament:** Solid, stable, practical, busy and constructive.	FIRE **Signs:** ♈ ♌ ♐ **Temperament:** Warm, eager, passionate and volatile.
AIR **Signs:** ♊ ♎ ♒ **Temperament:** Bright, sparkly, communicative and sociable.	WATER **Signs:** ♋ ♏ ♓ **Temperament:** Sensitive, creative, receptive and refreshing.

The Quality groups

CARDINAL
Signs: ♈ ♋ ♎ ♑
Your instinctive approach: The decision-makers of the Zodiac, you get things started and won't brook delays. Once you've set a project in motion, you're happy to delegate while you meet the next challenge.

FIXED
Signs: ♉ ♌ ♏ ♒
Your instinctive approach: You set your mind on a target and persist until you've achieved it. You may resist change, but you work hard.

MUTABLE
Signs: ♊ ♍ ♐ ♓
Your instinctive approach: You're brilliant at bringing people and ideas together. You love variety. Flexible and adaptable, you're innately versatile.

Aries

21 March – 20 April

As the sign that begins the astrological year, Aries represents fresh endeavours and all things new. Here is where the cosmic cycle starts, with your sign leading the way. No wonder, then, that you're impatient if you have to wait in line for something. Your natural inclination is to march straight to the front!

Not only does your sign lead the rest of the Zodiac, it's the first of the Fire signs: hot, passionate, enthusiastic and eager. Known as a "cardinal" sign (see pages 10–11), Aries is associated with activity. Being born into this group makes you a mover and a shaker. Traditionally, the symbol representing your sign stands for the horns of the ram, the creature said to embody the characteristics of Aries. But the glyph could just as easily be seen as the eyebrows and nose of a face, which is most apt as your sign rules the head.

Why you're so hot!

Driven by Mars, planet of energy and ambition, you're a natural-born leader and a trail-blazer. Outgoing and courageous, there's a fearless quality about you that others can't help but admire. Adventure always attracts you – wherever there is a place to explore, an ocean to sail or a mountain to conquer, there you'll be. If it's new, it's exciting; if it's daring, you'll find the challenge utterly irresistible.

Forever in a rush, for you, Aries, there is always so much to do and so little time to accomplish all that you have in mind. You're bursting with good ideas, and are a great organizer, although in truth you don't always finish what you begin.

Nevertheless, as the Zodiac's initiator, there's so much that simply wouldn't happen without your passionate and dynamic spark.

You and your ...

... CAREER

Competitive and self-motivated, you want to be at the cutting edge. Go for jobs that give quick returns and a fast turnaround: sales, sports, engineering or firefighting.

... HOME AND SOCIAL LIFE

Clean lines and no frills characterize your home. Gadgets please you, especially if they save you time. You love DIY, but if projects drag on, you're likely to lose interest. A sporty person, you adore the outdoors and love having a barbecue or playing soccer with the kids.

... HEALTH AND HAPPINESS

Tension headaches plague you, and your tendency to rush around predisposes you to accidental cuts, bruises and burns. Nevertheless, being physically active keeps you trim. Adventure holidays and winning at sports please you the most.

... LOVE LIFE

Born with huge amounts of sex appeal, you're a magnet to the opposite sex; but you love it when you get the thrill of the chase. Not surprising, then, that Aries tend to have several short-term liaisons before finding "the one".

Cosmic compatibility

So who turns you on, Aries?

EARTH SIGNS	*block your get-up-and-go*
TAURUS	slow burn
VIRGO	presents challenges
CAPRICORN	differing needs
FIRE SIGNS	*provide the perfect pairing*
ARIES	sizzling affair
LEO	robust romance
SAGITTARIUS	strong physical attraction
AIR SIGNS	*stimulate your fascination*
GEMINI	keeps you guessing
LIBRA	a tantalizing team
AQUARIUS	exciting experience
WATER SIGNS	*leave you floundering in the deep*
CANCER	emotionally clingy
SCORPIO	short-term passion
PISCES	demanding

EMBLEMS

birthstones:
garnet, diamond, bloodstone

colours:
red, scarlet, carmine

Taurus

21 April – 21 May

Yours is the second sign in the Zodiac line-up, and being second in line – a follower – is a position you feel most comfortable in. Unlike Aries, who comes immediately before you in the celestial year, you're not keen on leading the pack. Rather, like the bull that represents your sign, you're placid and patient. Until, that is, someone waves a red rag under your nose!

The symbol that represents Taurus resembles the head and horns of a bull, although some see it as depicting the shoulders and neck – the anatomical areas ruled by your sign. And it's true that, no matter how slight or slender you may be, you're capable of carrying more weight of responsibility on your shoulders than many other people. Your sign is ruled by Venus, goddess of love, looks, luck and all things luscious, so you are essentially receptive and feminine.

Why you're so dreamy!

Belonging to this sign means that you're sensual and pleasure-loving. Mellow and easygoing, you're delightful to be with. People love being in your company, and you'll always have many friends. This is because you make everyone feel so relaxed – and because they know that you're a great cook. You can always be relied on to provide an extra helping or three!

But you also give so much more besides. You're solid and sensible, and always prepared to roll up your sleeves and pitch in when someone needs a helping hand. A brilliant organizer – whether it's a child's birthday party, a house sale or a gala dinner – you know how to put a complicated situation together with stunning success. You attract good fortune, too, and you certainly have a magic touch when it comes to making money.

You and your ...

... CAREER

You like practical work, especially if it's also creative; and whatever you take on, you see through to the end (but only at your own pace). You're hardworking and dependable. Careers in property, banking and design are good choices.

... HOME AND SOCIAL LIFE

Security is top of your list. That, and a sense of luxury. You're drawn to classical styles in soft, earthy tones. For you, food is where the heart is, so the kitchen is your pride and joy. Entertaining friends and loved ones is one of your special delights.

... HEALTH AND HAPPINESS

The neck is your weakness and you're prone to sore throats. Taureans tend to put on weight easily, but as you adore music and dance, combine the two and exercise to your favourite CD to stay trim.

... LOVE LIFE

You can be a flirt, but you adore cuddles and like to be showered with compliments. You're choosy and give your heart only to a partner on whom you can rely. Once you do fall in love, you're steadfast and true.

Cosmic compatibility

So who leaves you breathless, Taurus?

EARTH SIGNS	*make your perfect partners*
TAURUS	caring and sharing
VIRGO	rock-solid
CAPRICORN	a lasting combination
AIR SIGNS	*feel too ethereal for your down-to-earth needs*
GEMINI	too changeable
LIBRA	compromise pays
AQUARIUS	jarringly unconventional
FIRE SIGNS	*are perhaps just too hot to handle*
ARIES	unsustainable
LEO	a superficial attraction
SAGITTARIUS	hard work
WATER SIGNS	*are in perfect harmony with you*
CANCER	the Earth moves for you
SCORPIO	either a hit or a miss
PISCES	inseparable

EMBLEMS

birthstones:
emerald, rose quartz, lapis lazuli

colours:
pink, light blue, pea green

Gemini

22 May – 22 June

The Heavenly Twins, the symbol for your sign, very much describe the duality of your make-up. With you, we get two of everything – or so it appears. Perhaps it's because you're so fast at what you do that you seem to be here, there and everywhere. Temperamentally, too, you can be up one minute and down the next. Gemini, you just love to keep us guessing!

Yours may be the third sign of the Zodiac but, coming after the ram and the bull, you're the first sign to be represented by a human form. And with Mercury, the messenger of the gods, as your ruler, is it any wonder, that Gemini is first and foremost associated with communication, travel and education? Quick to adapt, quick to grasp the nettle, quick to change your moods and opinions, your mind is constantly on the move, just like the Air – the element to which your sign belongs.

Why you're so breezy!

Gemini, you're a breath of fresh air! You're bright and cheerful and, being so witty, you're a gas. There isn't a subject you're not interested in. Nor one on which you haven't a comment to contribute. You're a huge asset at any gathering or dinner party with your sparkle and your endless anecdotes.

Although you're basically restless, once you learn to focus and concentrate, you can achieve twice as much as anyone else, and usually in half the time. You can be twice as lucky, twice as rich, twice as successful ...

Best of all, you're ever-youthful. Being taken for a teenager in your twenties may be frustrating, but looking twenty years younger in your sixties will make others wish they, too, had been born under your sign.

You and your ...

... CAREER

No-one can multi-task like you can, so variety is key. You need a workplace buzzing with intelligent ideas. Sales suits you, as do education and the media.

... HOME AND SOCIAL LIFE

Light, airy and modern – that's your kind of environment. You quickly tire of your decor, so you frequently change the look of your place, delighting in the latest interior fads. You're a sparkling party person – entertaining and being entertained are your favourite pastimes.

... HEALTH AND HAPPINESS

The chances are that if you injure yourself, you will hurt your limbs, especially your arms or hands. You are also prone to respiratory ailments – colds, coughs, asthma and bronchitis. Want to stay happy and healthy? Get plenty of sleep and lots of fresh air.

... LOVE LIFE

Monotony dulls your spirit, which is why you find committing yourself to one person for a whole lifetime a really big issue. But find someone who is tolerant, broad-minded and amusing, and you'll happily settle down.

Cosmic compatibility

So who blows you away, Gemini?

EARTH SIGNS	*clip your wings*
TAURUS	too down-to-earth
VIRGO	too serious
CAPRICORN	too focused
AIR SIGNS	*make an excellent match*
GEMINI	companionable couple
LIBRA	easygoing love
AQUARIUS	stimulating fun
FIRE SIGNS	*intrigue and engage you*
ARIES	an adventurous affair
LEO	magnetically attractive
SAGITTARIUS	surprisingly good
WATER SIGNS	*rain on your parade*
CANCER	too homely
SCORPIO	a struggle
PISCES	tears before bedtime

EMBLEMS

birthstones:
agate, tourmaline, citrine

colours:
pale yellow, white, magenta

Cancer

23 June – 23 July

Fourth in the Zodiac cycle, your sign is represented by the crab. This creature's crusty outer shell and soft inside perfectly illustrate your tender emotions, which you like to hide beneath a protective exterior.

Some say the symbol for Cancer resembles the nipping claws of the crab and, given your tenacious character, that analogy would certainly fit. Others say that the symbol represents the breasts. As Cancer is the most motherly and nurturing sign in the zodiac, this image, too, would seem apt – even more so as, astrologically, your sign is associated with the anatomical areas of the chest and stomach.

Water is the element group to which your sign belongs, enhancing your sensitivity and receptivity. But, above all, you are ruled by Earth's satellite, the shape-shifting Moon. Just as she waxes and wanes, so your moods and impressions are constantly in flux, responding sympathetically to the situation and the people you are with.

Why you're so needed!

Warm and caring, it's that super-sensitivity of yours that enables you to tune in instantly to other people's needs. And your superb memory never forgets a face or an important date, such as a friend's birthday.

Talking about the past is one of your favourite amusements, and you'll happily spend an evening with a special aunt reminiscing over the old times, or listening to an elderly neighbour chatting about her childhood. You're always there to lend an ear, to smile or to squeeze a hand.

In some situations you may be shy. Not, though, in business. You have a good head for finances, a nose for a bargain and an unerring eye for a collectable that one day could be worth a fortune.

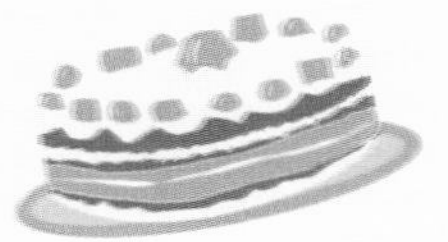

You and your ...

... CAREER

Your sharp memory is one of your assets, as this means you can remember facts and figures that others forget. It's handy in the teaching profession, financial sector or heritage industry. Cancers are happy in all kinds of domestic situations, from cooking through interior design to town-planning.

... HOME AND SOCIAL LIFE

If you're a true Cancer, your cosy home is the centre of your universe, and you love to decorate it in creams and cool greens. Nothing pleases you more than belonging to a tight-knit, loving family, and family celebrations are your favourite times.

... HEALTH AND HAPPINESS

Worry is your main hazard as it affects your stomach, causing nervous indigestion and nausea. For instant bliss, add aromatherapy oils to a hot tub and soak those cares away. Wonderful!

... LOVE LIFE

You're a romantic, but you're reticent in giving your heart. When you do find your soulmate, you're affectionate and supportive, and you make a devoted partner.

Cosmic compatibility

So who floats your boat, Cancer?

EARTH SIGNS	*provide a safe haven for you*
TAURUS	physically sublime
VIRGO	solid and secure
CAPRICORN	strong unit
AIR SIGNS	*are all froth and little substance*
GEMINI	little common ground
LIBRA	one-sided love
AQUARIUS	too unstructured
FIRE SIGNS	*tend to go over the top*
ARIES	steamy but short-lived
LEO	united through family love
SAGITTARIUS	heated to boiling point
WATER SIGNS	*are where you'll find mutual empathy*
CANCER	sexual fireworks
SCORPIO	a lasting passion
PISCES	loving and sweet

EMBLEMS

birthstones:
pearl, moonstone, chysocolla

colours:
silver, white, cerulean blue

Leo

24 July – 23 August

Since ancient times, Leo has been represented by a lion – the King of the Jungle: courageous, proud, dignified and aristocratic. These are the qualities that tradition assigns to Leo people, too.

The symbol for Leo depicts the lion's tail, although some say the circle symbolizes the heart. There is sense in this latter explanation, as, according to astrological lore, your sign is associated with the heart and the spine. The Sun is your planetary ruler. Golden and glorious, it imbues you with vitality, energy and creative power. And because your sign also belongs to the Fire element, you are doubly ardent, passionate and fiery. When you're angry, you roar like the proverbial King of the Beasts. But when you're happy – which is your more usual disposition – the sunshine from your eyes can light up an entire room.

Why you're so sunny!

Colourful, vibrant and dramatic, you draw people to you in the same way that they are drawn to a bright light. This is just as well, as your favourite place is centre-stage, with admirers surrounding you.

You're a natural extrovert – attractive and sexy, with an infectious laugh and a wonderful love of living life to the full – meaning that there's nothing you enjoy more than a good party. And because you were born with sunshine in your soul, you can't help but inspire and motivate those you meet, making you an excellent boss and a stimulating mentor.

All Leos are born with a code of honour stamped on to their hearts. This means that you stand up for justice and truth. Not only are you hugely generous toward those you love, but being innately magnanimous means that you can't simply walk by and ignore anyone genuinely in need.

You and your ...

... CAREER

You're at your happiest in a position of authority. The world of entertainment is an ideal career avenue for you, as you're drawn to the spotlight. Fashion and beauty also attract you – these satisfy your love of luxury and glamour.

... HOME AND SOCIAL LIFE

There's always a "wow" factor associated with the Leo house. You like to impress with opulent furnishings and rich colours, often accenting with reds and golds. Mirrors are everywhere – after all, Leos are a little vain! You're a party animal and enjoy throwing lavish gatherings.

... HEALTH AND HAPPINESS

Leos push themselves to the max, placing strain on their hearts and spines. Taking a more balanced approach will still make you smile but help you live longer, too!

... LOVE LIFE

Like all lions, you like to give chase, but when you've caught your heart's desire, you'll withdraw your claws and settle into contented togetherness. Generous and big-hearted, you give yourself completely to the one you love.

Cosmic compatibility

So who lights your fire, Leo?

EARTH SIGNS	*can stomp on your feelings*
TAURUS	fun for a while
VIRGO	picky, picky
CAPRICORN	too stuffy
AIR SIGNS	*stimulate your desire*
GEMINI	enthusiastic love
LIBRA	indulgent lovers
AQUARIUS	a delicious hit
FIRE SIGNS	*share a special bond with you*
ARIES	hot love
LEO	a fiery affair
SAGITTARIUS	a passion that lasts
WATER SIGNS	*can sometimes work creatively*
CANCER	warm domesticity
SCORPIO	too intense
PISCES	imaginative

EMBLEMS

birthstones:
ruby, amber, chrysolite

colours:
gold, flame orange, sun yellow

Virgo

24 August – 23 September

Sixth in the Zodiac cycle, Virgo is the second sign represented by a human figure. In the corn maiden, who carries a sheaf of corn in her arms, we have an image of the harvest – golden, fecund, ripe, wholesome and giving. Here, we see the notion of the provider, an instinct that permeates through all members of your sign.

Enhancing your practical nature is the fact that Virgo belongs to the Earth element: solid, sensible, reliable. With your feet firmly planted on the ground, you are one of life's supreme realists. Clear-thinking Mercury, ruler of the mind, is your guiding planet, which sharpens your intellect and imparts shrewdness and good judgment to your decisions. Your symbol is complex and its imagery not readily decipherable. Some say that it brings to mind the form of a seated woman with her legs crossed at the ankles – a reflection of Virgo's coyness. Others recognize in the symbol the coils of the intestines, which is the anatomical area associated with this sign.

Why you're such a hero!

Need a friend? Look no further than Virgo. Belonging to this sign means that you're there for other people. No matter how difficult their problem, how messy their emotions or how complicated their situation, you will drop everything to run to their rescue. Practical, logical and straightforward, your kind heart goes out to anyone who cries for help.

You give your undivided attention to whatever you're doing and whoever you're with. And because you like things just so, you're always prepared to go that extra mile. When others tire, you'll be putting those finishing touches to the arrangements that make the difference between a winner and an also-ran.

You and your ...

... CAREER

Yours is the sign of service, and many Virgos gravitate toward the medical and caring professions. You also have a keen eye for detail and superb organizational skills.

... HOME AND SOCIAL LIFE

Noted for their quiet tastes, Virgos go for understated, comfortable, practical homes, decorated in earthy tones. Tidiness pleases you, and hygiene is top of your list. Socially, you enjoy cosy dinner parties with intelligent conversation and card games or quizzes for entertainment.

... HEALTH AND HAPPINESS

Virgos tend to suffer with intestinal problems – so try to eat a natural, organic diet. You're a bit of a hypochondriac, and need gentle exercise to release those feel-good chemicals and lift your spirits.

... LOVE LIFE

Clever people turn you on – you put brains before beauty. You need to be sure of your feelings before you commit, so love often grows out of a friendship. To the one you love, you're not only faithful, reliable and true, but wise and witty, too.

Cosmic compatibility

So, Virgo, who leaves you panting for more?

EARTH SIGNS	*could provide your winning match*
TAURUS	a deep attraction
VIRGO	sympathetic feelings
CAPRICORN	solid gold

AIR SIGNS	*may prove destabilizing*
GEMINI	too glib
LIBRA	disappointing
AQUARIUS	cool and detached

FIRE SIGNS	*can be hard to handle*
ARIES	different directions
LEO	too extravagant
SAGITTARIUS	a restless partnership

WATER SIGNS	*make a mutually rewarding combination*
CANCER	total commitment
SCORPIO	mutual respect
PISCES	compassionate but chaotic

EMBLEMS

birthstones:
jasper, peridot, sardonyx

colours:
green, terracotta, saffron

Libra

24 September – 23 October

Everything about you speaks of equilibrium. For a start, your sign is represented by the balance, which some call the scales of justice. It's an appropriate symbol, because you constantly find yourself weighing up the pros and cons of different life situations. Plus, you can always be relied upon for a balanced opinion.

We see balance again in the Zodiacal position of your sign. Being in seventh place, Libra is poised at the mid-way point of the cycle, beginning around the time of the Northern hemisphere's Autumn Equinox (22 September), which marks the tipping point of the seasons and the start of the second half of the astrological year.

Even anatomically there is a reference to balance in that, astrologically, Libra corresponds to the kidneys – the two organs that filter toxins out of the body to restore our internal equilibrium.

Air, cool and light, is your sign's element – and this is just how you like to present yourself. And aptly, too, Air is also the medium through which we speak our thoughts. In any situation you, Libra, seem to know exactly what to say, meaning you're always comfortable in social settings.

Why you're so heavenly!

First and foremost you're ruled by Venus, the goddess of love – and of beauty, looks and luck, too. No wonder you're so attractive! Venus endows you with grace and poise, and also with exquisite taste. Appearance matters to you, which is why, no matter what you're doing, you're always perfectly polished.

You strive for harmony and enjoy the finer things in life – music, sculpture, art, photography and architecture. Cultured, refined and gentle-mannered, you're a thoughtful companion, and when you are entertaining friends you know exactly how to make sure they relax and have a good time.

You and your ...

... CAREER

Given your inclination toward indecision, choosing a career is a big challenge for you. You're diplomatic, so judicial occupations, advisory positions or PR would suit. Your elegance draws you to the fashion or design industries.

... HOME AND SOCIAL LIFE

The Libran home is quintessentially stylish. You like balance and symmetry, and favour shades of cool or earthy green. Socially, you enjoy dinner parties; you're a gracious host and an amusing guest. Concerts and comedies make you happy.

... HEALTH AND HAPPINESS

Your sign rules the kidneys and bladder and, when your system is thrown out of balance, this is where things go wrong. Tennis, yoga, ballroom dancing or t'ai chi are great ways for you to stay fit.

... LOVE LIFE

Libra governs relationships, and you were born to be in love. Charming and easy-going, you attract admirers like bees to honey. The one you choose will be beautiful, well-mannered and able to look good at all times.

Cosmic compatibility

So who pulls all your strings, Libra?

EARTH SIGNS	*may hold you back*
TAURUS	hit and miss
VIRGO	critically correct
CAPRICORN	overly organized
AIR SIGNS	*are where you'll feel most in tune*
GEMINI	cool, balanced and beautiful
LIBRA	delightful duo
AQUARIUS	ultimate elegance
FIRE SIGNS	*make a good match that works well*
ARIES	an attraction of opposites
LEO	good friends and true
SAGITTARIUS	guaranteed understanding
WATER SIGNS	*can dampen your spirits*
CANCER	sweet but short
SCORPIO	worlds apart
PISCES	too needy

EMBLEMS

birthstones:
opal, rose quartz, marble

colours:
rose pink, pastel blue, jade green

Scorpio

24 October – 22 November

Represented by the scorpion, yours is the sign of power. You may not say much – remember, scorpions have no voice – but there's a maelstrom of activity deep inside. And because you're ruled by Pluto, the secretive god of the underworld, you're not only deep, you can be pretty unfathomable, too.

Water is your element, but don't imagine your emotions as torrents or mighty waterfalls. To describe your feelings more accurately, think instead of a glassy lake, whose mirrored stillness on the surface belies the turbulent and dangerous undercurrents swirling powerfully below.

Scorpio's symbol is the upraised tail of the scorpion, with the deadly sting at its point, ready to take aim. Recognize the symbolism? Incidentally, the Ancients portrayed your sign not as a scorpion, but as an eagle, soaring high above the material plane, a symbol of transcendence. It's a fitting image as Scorpio is associated with transformation and rebirth.

Why you're so irresistible!

You're a sexy creature; there's something dark and sultry about you. Focused and intense, you exude an air of mystery that others find tantalizing and alluring.

Mentally and emotionally, there's an elemental power about you that makes you one of the strongest people in the universe. With your forceful determination, coupled with your extraordinary endurance, if anyone can achieve mind over matter, you can. Once you've set your sights on something, nothing will stand in your way until you get what you want.

You're brilliant at research, and at unearthing facts and information – you, Scorpio, are the determined detective of the Sun signs! And when it comes to problem-solving, there are few who can outdo you.

You and your ...

... CAREER

Whether you're involved in forensic science, are rooting out information or are digging for buried treasure, precision is your forte. Engineering, psychoanalysis, surgery – even butchery – suit Scorpio's precise and enquiring mind.

... HOME AND SOCIAL LIFE

You love a moody environment with rich burgundies and sumptuous fabrics, or stark monochrome tones softened by dimmed lighting. Socially, you prefer a few good friends to a crowd of acquaintances.

... HEALTH AND HAPPINESS

You're pretty robust health-wise, mainly because you don't believe in being ill. If it does happen, ill-health is likely to affect your reproductive organs, or your bladder or bowels. Nevertheless, mind over matter will keep you happy.

... LOVE LIFE

Often described as sexy and seductive, you don't go in for emotional games – although you are prone to jealousy. Loyalty, honesty and trust are key in your relationships. When you give your heart, it is for ever.

Cosmic compatibility

So who has the magic formula for you, Scorpio?

EARTH SIGNS	*make a fruitful combination in so many ways*
TAURUS	deeply emotional
VIRGO	committed
CAPRICORN	steamy love
AIR SIGNS	*can prove frustrating for you*
GEMINI	untenable
LIBRA	too diffuse
AQUARIUS	uncomfortable
FIRE SIGNS	*will make steam come out of your ears!*
ARIES	passionate but combustible
LEO	drama and tears
SAGITTARIUS	ships passing in the night
WATER SIGNS	*ease you into your comfort zone*
CANCER	a bond for life
SCORPIO	plenty of passion
PISCES	intensely loving

EMBLEMS

birthstones:
jasper, malachite, topaz

colours:
claret red, aubergine, black

Sagittarius

23 November – 21 December

Just as your sign is symbolized by the centaur – half-man, half-beast – so there is a duality in your character. No other sign of the Zodiac combines the physical and the mental like Sagittarius. Like a centaur, you gallop through life, travelling far and wide, picking up new experiences and wisdom en route.

Sagittarius comes from the Latin word for "arrow", hence the symbol for your sign. Just as the centaur-archer takes his bow and looks skyward, so you set your sights on the big vista. Often, you shoot your ideas way off into the distance. And often, because of your highly tuned intuition, you hit the bull's-eye full on.

Being a member of the Fire element endows you with a passion for living life to the full. The world is a big and colourful place, and you want to gallop ahead to explore every last fascinating part of it.

Why you're so lovable!

You're a happy-go-lucky, likeable soul. Generous, genial and fun-loving, people always find you easy to get along with and enjoy being your friend. Little seems to dent your exuberance or to diminish your enthusiasm for life. Even when events conspire against you and life knocks you down, you just get up, dust yourself off and march eagerly onward in search of your next big adventure with a smile on your face. And you have no trouble finding followers. That natural exuberance of yours seems to gather people to you as to a magnet, firing their imagination and warming their hearts with your joie-de-vivre.

You may be either sporty or bookish, or perhaps both. But whatever you do, good fortune seems to follow you around. And no wonder: with Jupiter, bringer of luck, as your life-guide, you invariably find yourself in just the right place at just the right time. Go ahead, Sagittarius, just keep shooting for those stars!

You and your ...

... CAREER

Versatile and adaptable, the world is your oyster. You're drawn to political organizations, lecture halls, legal offices and media studios. But you're also active, so you're just as at home in the world of sports or in travel.

... HOME AND SOCIAL LIFE

Your rooms may not be tidy, your chairs won't match and your surfaces won't be dust-free, but your home will be comfortable. You love to pick up an item of furniture from a flea market and turn it into a treasure. You have masses of friends and enjoy informal gatherings.

... HEALTH AND HAPPINESS

You love fine wine and good food – a disaster for your liver and waistline. Hiking and running are great therapies for you, getting you fit *and* out into the fresh air.

... LOVE LIFE

You flirt, you tell jokes, you turn on all that charm and you like to play the field; but you're also passionate, honest, kind-hearted and fun. Find someone who shares the same outlook and you'll make a great team.

Cosmic compatibility

So who does the business for you, Sagittarius?

EARTH SIGNS	*can put out your fire*
TAURUS	different desires
VIRGO	too many rules
CAPRICORN	uncomfortably formal
AIR SIGNS	*are fabulously frothy*
GEMINI	fickle fun
LIBRA	romantic delight
AQUARIUS	shared passions
FIRE SIGNS	*are super-complementary for you*
ARIES	sensationally scorching
LEO	passionate love
SAGITTARIUS	deep understanding
WATER SIGNS	*may douse your ardour*
CANCER	sensitive
SCORPIO	too deep
PISCES	tender but troubled

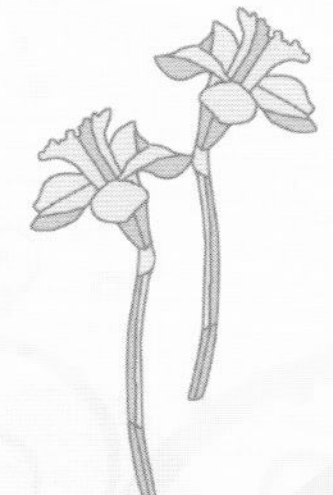

EMBLEMS

birthstones:
turquoise, lapis lazuli, topaz

colours:
purple, royal blue, magenta

Capricorn

22 December – 20 January

No wonder you feel that you were born with an old head on young shoulders – you're ruled by Saturn, the taskmaster of the heavens and the Father of Time. Duty and responsibility are Capricorn's watchwords, which means that you work hard for your living. Your sign is symbolized by the sure-footed mountain goat, who unflinchingly climbs the precipitous crags to reach the very top. Yours is the sign of ambition and eventual success.

Capricorn is associated with the Earth element, which gives you that solidity and constancy. It also means that, while reaching the summit is your ultimate goal, strong foundations are crucial to your sense of purpose and well-being. Once established, they give you the courage and determination to succeed.

Why you fly so high!

The best thing about you, Capricorn, is that you never give up. Obstacles that get in other people's way, or that would defeat a lesser mortal are, for you, simply a challenge that your thrive on. One way or another, you're determined to find a way around that problem and come out triumphant in the end. And invariably, you do just that – and with flying colours, too.

It may seem as though the weight of the world is resting on your shoulders, but then you surprise everyone with a dry sense of humour that is utterly priceless. No-one can quite floor an opponent with the sort of brilliant one-liner that you come up with so spontaneously. Subtle and wry, you keep your audience rolling in the aisles!

Old age holds no terrors for you because you simply blossom with age. The older you get, the more your mind and health improve – and the younger you look. Are we envious? You bet we are!

You and your ...

... CAREER

Dutiful and industrious, you take your work seriously. Business and administration are good avenues for you, as are engineering and economics. Your eye is always on the top rung of the ladder, which you reach by sheer hard work.

... HOME AND SOCIAL LIFE

You give time and effort to making your home gleam; you have an eye for quality and won't flinch at expensive price tags. You're choosy about your friends, moving only in the "right" circles. Mixing business with pleasure is what you do best.

... HEALTH AND HAPPINESS

Capricorns have a reputation for longevity, but bones, skin and hair are your weak links. A good skincare routine and cycling, walking and golf, are ideal for you, as are stretching and Pilates.

... LOVE LIFE

You take a serious approach to relationships, and you don't believe in flirting. The chances are that you'll meet your lifelong partner at work – someone respectable and earnest. To this tower of strength you'll remain loyal and true.

Cosmic compatibility

So who holds the key to your heart, Capricorn?

EARTH SIGNS	*let you know where you stand*
TAURUS	solid and true
VIRGO	deep trust
CAPRICORN	best of friends

AIR SIGNS	*are better partners in business than in love*
GEMINI	too distracting
LIBRA	lightweight
AQUARIUS	on different plains

FIRE SIGNS	*are too volatile for comfort*
ARIES	lacks maturity
LEO	has merit
SAGITTARIUS	too casual

WATER SIGNS	*make up a dream team*
CANCER	fabulous feelings
SCORPIO	potent power
PISCES	enduring fascination

EMBLEMS

birthstones:
jet, onyx, sapphire

colours:
navy blue, indigo, forest green

Aquarius

21 January – 19 February

Aquarius is the most sociable of the Sun signs, associated with friendship and ruling over gatherings, such as clubs, societies and committees. Open-minded and objective, Aquarians are renowned for their tolerance, their sense of fair play and their natural acceptance of other people's quirks and foibles. Above all, they believe in equality.

Aquarius is an Air sign, and the jagged waves of its symbol represent not water, as you may think, but light – radiation or electrical impulses that pass through the ether. This sign is often depicted as a woman pouring water. But what she is truly pouring is not water, but information – intelligence sourced from the fountain of knowledge. It's altogether rather appropriate really, as Aquarius is the sign of the higher intellect. Aquarians are far-sighted and ahead of their time. Described as the visionary of the Zodiac, Aquarius rules over hopes and wishes, and looks to the future and beyond.

Why you're so "out there"!

Ever wondered why you're so deliciously different, why your ideas are so extraordinary, and why you keep asking questions other people just haven't the imagination to have thought of? It's because you're ruled by Uranus!

This planet represents electricity, lightning bolts and revolution. Uranus breaks rules, flouts convention and thumbs its nose at the world. Unpredictable, unconventional and a true non-conformist, being an Aquarius makes you astrology's wild child. You're not just fun, you're totally original, highly inventive and completely refreshing to be around. Sometimes zany and often misunderstood, you're streets ahead of everyone else and always ready to experiment – even if your exploits can land you in very hot water!

You and your ...

... CAREER

Scientific research and engineering are ideal choices for you, as are alternative careers, such as complementary medicine. Social work satisfies your conscience.

... HOME AND SOCIAL LIFE

You like ultra-modern lines and bold colours. Your home is stocked with high-tech gadgets, which will give visitors all sorts of unusual talking points. You enjoy a wide social network and are always there for a friend in need. Intelligent and entertaining, you're great in a crowd and are valued because you're so understanding.

... HEALTH AND HAPPINESS

Exercise-wise, go for low-impact aerobics – it's easy on your legs (you're known for weak ankles!) and good for your circulation. Having something to believe in is what gladdens your soul.

... LOVE LIFE

A stimulating conversation will steal your heart faster than good looks. Your love is unconditional, but you insist on holding your independence and cannot abide jealousy. You are as unconventional in love as you are by nature.

Cosmic compatibility

So who leaves you swooning, Aquarius?

AIR SIGNS	*sing from your song book*
GEMINI	swept off your feet
LIBRA	elegant couple
AQUARIUS	true understanding
FIRE SIGNS	*set you alight with a perfect blend of spirits*
ARIES	sizzling possiblities
LEO	opposites attract
SAGITTARIUS	explosive action
EARTH SIGNS	*can provide stability*
TAURUS	a long-term friendship
VIRGO	intellectually stimulating
CAPRICORN	best as a working partnership
WATER SIGNS	*could leave you gasping for oxygen*
CANCER	stuck in their ways
SCORPIO	too controlling
PISCES	different emotional needs

EMBLEMS

birthstones:
amethyst, blue sapphire

colours:
blue, green, silvery-purple

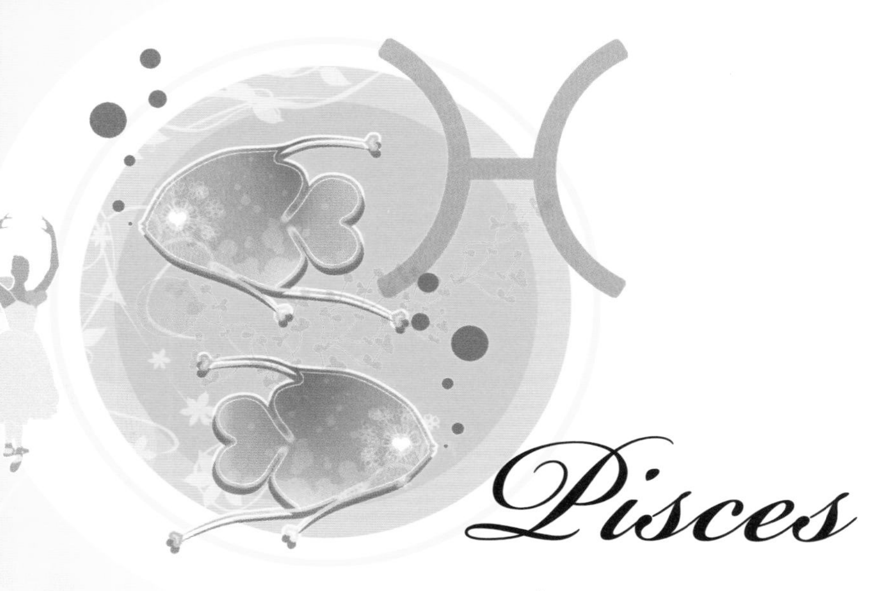

Pisces

20 February – 20 March

As the twelfth sign of the Zodiac, Pisces completes the Sun-signs cycle. It is said that in its journey around the Zodiac, the Sun picks up the salient characteristics of each sign it travels through. By the time it reaches you, Pisces, the Sun has quite a collection of human stories in all the hues of the rainbow for you to take on board. No wonder, then, that you know what other people are feeling – you're exquisitely compassionate and empathetic toward your fellow humans.

Pisces is associated with the Water element, highlighting your sensitivity and your tendency to react emotionally to the challenges of life. In astrological terms, the sign of Pisces corresponds to the feet, and your feet are the area of your body in which you experience the most physical problems.

Ruled by Neptune, the sea god and guardian of the oceans, yours is the sign of spirituality. Pisces is symbolized by two fish joined together but swimming in opposite directions, representing the temporary union of body and soul which, in time, must inevitably pull apart.

Why you're so wise!

As a Pisces, you believe the best of everyone and see beauty everywhere you look. Gentle and caring, you have a ready sympathy for anyone in need of comfort. Your deep understanding of human nature makes you a wonderful friend and advisor. You're always there with a kind word. And if that isn't enough, there's a cheering bowl of chicken soup to follow!

Your spiritual nature means that you are blessed with flashes of insight and wonderful vision. Using words, paint or music, you can make others believe that a better world exists. Only you can conjure up the sort of magic that has the power to transport others to a higher plane.

You and your ...

... CAREER

Medicine and the arts (particuarly music and literature) are a great draw. Whatever you do, avoid stressful working conditions. Congenial surroundings and co-operative colleagues are essential to your well-being.

... HOME AND SOCIAL LIFE

Home for you is a cluttered but eclectic mix of styles, imaginatively put together to create a soft and desirable ambience that is altogether romantic. Blues dominate, with either views that look out over water or accessories associated with the sea.

... HEALTH AND HAPPINESS

Pisces are prone to foot troubles – flat feet, in-growing toe nails, bunions and gout, to name but a few! Swimming is wonderfully therapeutic for you and so is ballet, despite your problem feet.

... LOVE LIFE

As the ultimate romantic, it's roses around the door and happy-ever-afters that fill your dreams. You're tender and giving, but you can be clingy, which is why you thrive best with a strong, supportive partner at your side.

Cosmic compatibility

So who presses all your buttons, Pisces?

EARTH SIGNS	*give you fabulous grounding*
TAURUS	winning formula
VIRGO	powerful exchange
CAPRICORN	compassionate caring
AIR SIGNS	*could take you way out of your depth*
GEMINI	fantasy land
LIBRA	delicious but unreal
AQUARIUS	open-ended
FIRE SIGNS	*can boil you dry*
ARIES	exhausting
LEO	demanding
SAGITTARIUS	short-term inspiration
WATER SIGNS	*offer a shared destiny*
CANCER	laid-back loving
SCORPIO	mesmerizing romance
PISCES	dreamy bliss

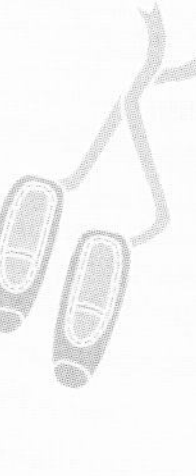

EMBLEMS

birthstones:
aquamarine, coral, chrysolite

colours:
violet, lavender, sea green

Predicting the Future

Many happy returns! Have you ever heard someone say that on a friend's birthday? And have you ever wondered, who or what is it that returns? Simple – it's the Sun. In astrological terms, the Sun travels through all twelve signs over twelve months returning, on your birthday, to the same point in the heavens where it was at the moment you were born. So a "return" denotes a whole revolution of the Sun and therefore a complete year of your life.

From this point on your birthday, the Sun starts off on a fresh journey and thus sets in motion the cycle of events that will take the next twelve months to complete.

Beginning at Aries and ending with Pisces, there are twelve signs of the Zodiac. Each sign describes a set of characteristics, personality traits and particular interests. For example, courageous Aries takes a keen interest in sports. Being first in the Zodiac cycle makes Aries something of a pushy sign, but it does mean that Aries people are keen to break new ground and lead the way. Gemini, on the other hand, is more cerebral. Matters of the mind, communication and social affairs are the principal preoccupations of this sign of the Zodiac.

As the Sun travels from sign to sign, it switches your attention to those aspects associated with the sign it is in at that time. So, in one month you may find that financial affairs predominate because that month's sign has rulership over money. Then, as the Sun moves out of that sign and into the next, it could be your domestic life that heats up, as family or property matters become the new leading preoccupations in your life for that particular month. Just as each sign influences the characteristics of the people born at that time of year, so it also affects what we think about and the actions we take.

This information empowers us to work with the Zodiac so that we can exploit its influences to our best advantage – planning when to take action and when to sit back and enjoy. As we know that the Sun spends just over four weeks in each sign, it is possible to work out, starting from your birthday, and in relation to your sign, which issues are likely to come up for you over the course of a year and, moreover, at what point in the year these affairs will be demanding your attention. Usually you would need an astrologer to map out these influences for you, but turn over the page to discover how to work them out for yourself.

Working with the Wheel of Time

On the following pages you will find a Zodiac Wheel of Time, divided into twelve sectors called astrological "houses". Conventionally, the houses are set into a wheel, or clock face, moving in an anticlockwise direction, starting with the sequence at the point on the dial that corresponds to 9 o'clock. This is House 1. The next sector contains House 2, and so on until we reach House 12.

Each house deals with a specific set of circumstances, subject areas, characteristics and associations. These, in short, are the salient matters flagged up as the Sun passes through this area, which will preoccupy your mind at that time of year. Your personal cycle begins when the Sun moves into your Zodiac sign; that is, when your Zodiac sign moves into House 1 on the clock face.

Here's what to do

Photocopy the wheel, then on your copy, starting at House 1 and using the details opposite, write the name of your sign and its dates in the box on the outer ring of the dial. Move anticlockwise to House 2 and here write the name and dates of the astrological sign that comes after yours. Write in all the sign details, in sequence.

THE ZODIAC YEAR	
♈ **Aries**	21 March–20 April
♉ **Taurus**	21 April–21 May
♊ **Gemini**	22 May–22 June
♋ **Cancer**	23 June–23 July
♌ **Leo**	24 July–23 August
♍ **Virgo**	24 August–23 September
♎ **Libra**	24 September–23 October
♏ **Scorpio**	24 October–22 November
♐ **Sagittarius**	23 November–21 December
♑ **Capricorn**	22 December–20 January
♒ **Aquarius**	21 January–19 February
♓ **Pisces**	20 February–20 March

On the date that the Sun leaves your sign, it will move anticlockwise into the next house, shifting your attention to the new set of issues represented there. One month later, the Sun will move again, turning the spotlight on to new preoccupations, and so on. Anticipating in this way the Sun's movement through the houses gives you a month-by-month advance glimpse of what situations are likely to arise through the year ahead, and how you are likely to deal with them – positively or negatively.

Highlighted houses show your most supportive times of year, when the Sun is in a sign from your Element group (see pages 10–11)

Sign:
Date:

career, status, achievements, ambition, employers, fathe authority figures, public im success and failure, ski hair, teeth, bones, kne walls, ceiling, roof

responsib

slyly

Sign:
Date:

friends, colleagues, social life, teamwork, life aims, groups, clubs, associations, high-tech equipment, airports, electrical wiring, blood circulation, ankles

inventively

rebelliously

11

Sign:
Date:

privacy, health matters, fears and phobias, imagination, subconscious, escapism, crime, institutions, hospitals, secrets, sadness, tiredness, feet, shoes

intuitively

clingingly

12

Sign:
Date:

fresh starts, new beginnings, your appearance, your health, your interests, adventure, taking action, your attitudes, head, eyes, mouth, hair, gates, doors, entrances

courageously

aggressively

1

Sign:
Date:

money, income, possessions, spending, bank, indulgences, ease, comfort, benefits, flower garden, florist, waiting room, the neck, throat, nose, ears, furniture, bedroom

kindly

lazily

2

3

incerely

telligently

rrespondence, telephone calls, blings, neighbours, acquiring owledge, communication uipment, school, local urneys, visits, limbs, gs, stairs, alleyways, your street

gn:
ate:

- matters arising
- positive response
- negative response
- House number

Making the Future Work for You

In tracking the Sun around the Zodiac Wheel of Time, houses 1, 5 and 9 have been highlighted. These show which dates are particularly supportive times of year for you because the Sun is in a sign that shares your Element group (see page 11). But when are you likely to earn more money or fall in love? When should you apply for a new job, redecorate your home, take extra care of your health? When does destiny decree that you'll find success at work, locate your dream house, travel around the world, marry or have a baby?

To try to answer some of these questions does require a professional astrologer, but there are ways that you can tune into opportunities, open your mind to possibilities, prepare for eventualities and give Fate a nudge in the ribs. It's all about timing. And timing is what astrology is all about!

Keeping in mind the affairs of each House and your responses to events, go back to the Zodiac Wheel of Time and, starting from your birthday, apply the information given in the table opposite to the house associations (the first month is your birth month, the second month is the month after that, and so on).

The best time to ...

Birthday month	*make new resolutions and put fresh strategies in place to improve your life, work, love and health*
2nd month	*focus on money, settle debts, ask for a raise, attend to business, file papers*
3rd month	*network, catch up with neighbourhood issues, visit friends and loved ones*
4th month	*concentrate on the home and family, DIY, redecorate, garden, move into a new home*
5th month	*relax, conceive a baby, travel, take up a new hobby, meet someone special*
6th month	*have health checks, improve your diet and fitness, get organized, apply for a new job*
7th month	*find a new business partner, sign contracts, marry*
8th month	*sort out business affairs, start a new savings scheme, get more intimate with that special someone*
9th month	*travel, contact people far away, advance your skills, apply to university, launch a PR campaign, think global!*
10th month	*go for promotion, get yourself noticed, enjoy your success*
11th month	*be sociable, join a club, make influential friends, re-think your goals*
12th month	*slow down, think about your health, pamper yourself, take time out, sleep!*

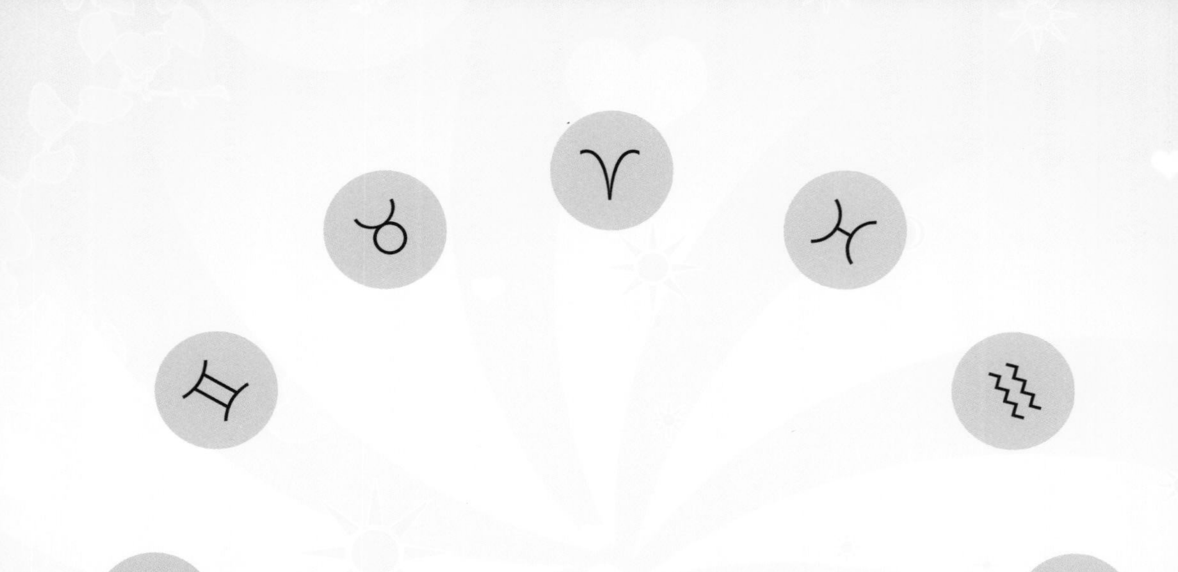

ASTROLOGY OF THE MOON

MOON SIGNS

Introducing Moon Sign Astrology

Most people know what sign of the Zodiac they belong to. Saying that you're a Gemini, a Leo or a Capricorn, for example, is pointing out in which sign the Sun was located at the time you were born. Very few people, however, know what sign the Moon was in on the day of their birth. And yet our Moon sign is just as important as our Sun sign, if not more so, because it is our Moon sign that reveals our innermost feelings and emotions.

As well as describing your feelings, your Moon sign can tell you about your deepest drives, your needs and desires, your reactions and personal sensitivities. It reflects how you interact with other people, what sorts of relationships you're likely to form, and how you come across emotionally. Your Moon sign will highlight your expectations, your dreams and hopes, what makes you feel good, what nurtures you and in what things or people you find the greatest comfort.

The Moon in Taurus, for example, will endow you with very different emotional characteristics from, say, the Moon in Sagittarius. In Taurus, the Moon strengthens and stabilizes the feelings. A person born with this Moon seeks permanence and security in his or her life. This is a very different story from that of the happy-go-lucky individual born under a Sagittarian Moon. This person would run a mile rather than be tied down.

So, each sign the Moon travels through will "colour" your emotions with its own distinctive characteristics and qualities. But because the Moon moves quickly through the Zodiac, staying for just two-and-a-quarter days in each sign, many of us normally use an expert astrologer to find the exact position of the Moon for our time of birth, thinking that this is not something we can do for ourselves.

However, over the following few pages, you will find three charts that will enable you to calculate your Moon sign yourself. The first chart (see pages 72–3) helps you to work out which sign the Moon was in during the month of your birth. The second chart (see page 74) adjusts this calculation for the precise day of your birth, enabling you to find out how much further around the wheel you need to travel for an accurate reading. The third chart (see page 75) is the final step and combines what you've learned in charts 1 and 2 to work out your Moon sign.

How to Find Your Moon Sign

Moon Chart 1: *The Moon's location on the first day of each month*

YEAR OF BIRTH			JAN	FEB	MAR	APR	MAY	JUN
1958	1977	1996	♉	♋	♋	♍	♎	♐
1959	1978	1997	♎	♏	♐	♑	♒	♈
1960	1979	1998	♒	♈	♈	♊	♋	♌
1961	1980	1999	♊	♌	♌	♎	♏	♑
1962	1981	2000	♏	♐	♑	♒	♈	♉
1963	1982	2001	♓	♉	♉	♋	♌	♎
1964	1983	2002	♌	♍	♎	♏	♐	♒
1965	1984	2003	♐	♑	♒	♓	♉	♊
1966	1985	2004	♈	♊	♊	♌	♍	♏
1967	1986	2005	♍	♏	♏	♑	♒	♓
1968	1987	2006	♑	♓	♓	♉	♊	♌
1969	1988	2007	♉	♋	♋	♍	♎	♐
1970	1989	2008	♎	♐	♐	♒	♓	♉
1971	1990	2009	♓	♈	♉	♊	♋	♍
1972	1991	2010	♋	♍	♍	♎	♐	♑
1973	1992	2011	♏	♑	♑	♓	♈	♊
1974	1993	2012	♈	♉	♊	♌	♍	♎
1975	1994	2013	♌	♎	♎	♐	♑	♓
1976	1995	2014	♑	♒	♓	♈	♉	♋

Run your finger down the columns on the far left of this chart to find the year in which you were born. Look across from that line until you reach your month of birth. Make a note of the symbol representing the Moon sign in that month, then turn over the page to the next chart.

JUL	AUG	SEP	OCT	NOV	DEC
♑	♒	♈	♉	♋	♌
♉	♋	♌	♍	♏	♐
♍	♏	♑	♒	♈	♉
♒	♈	♉	♊	♌	♍
♊	♌	♎	♏	♐	♑
♏	♐	♒	♓	♉	♊
♓	♉	♋	♌	♍	♎
♌	♍	♏	♐	♒	♓
♐	♒	♓	♈	♊	♋
♉	♊	♌	♍	♎	♐
♍	♏	♐	♑	♓	♈
♑	♓	♈	♊	♋	♌
♊	♋	♍	♎	♐	♑
♎	♐	♑	♒	♈	♉
♓	♈	♊	♋	♍	♎
♋	♍	♏	♐	♑	♒
♏	♑	♓	♈	♉	♋
♈	♉	♋	♌	♎	♏
♌	♎	♏	♑	♒	♈

THE TWELVE MOON SIGNS

♈ Aries

♉ Taurus

♊ Gemini

♋ Cancer

♌ Leo

♍ Virgo

♎ Libra

♏ Scorpio

♐ Sagittarius

♑ Capricorn

♒ Aquarius

♓ Pisces

Moon Chart 2: *The number of Moon signs to add on*

Look at the chart below and find the day of the month on which you were born (1 if you were born on the first of the month, 2 for the second, and so on). The number to the right of that day tells you how many extra Zodiac signs you need to add on from the sign you were given in Moon Chart 1.

YOU WERE BORN ON THIS DAY:	ADD THIS MANY SIGNS:	YOU WERE BORN ON THIS DAY:	ADD THIS MANY SIGNS:
1	0	16	7
2	1	17	7
3	1	18	8
4	1	19	8
5	2	20	9
6	2	21	9
7	3	22	10
8	3	23	10
9	4	24	10
10	4	25	11
11	5	26	11
12	5	27	0
13	5	28	0
14	6	29	1
15	6	30	1
		31	2

Moon Chart 3: *Identifying your Moon sign*

Here is the Zodiac wheel containing the twelve signs. Put your finger on the sign you were allocated in Moon Chart 1. Now, moving clockwise, count on the extra number of signs you were given in Moon Chart 2. The sign you arrive at is the sign the Moon was in on the day you were born.

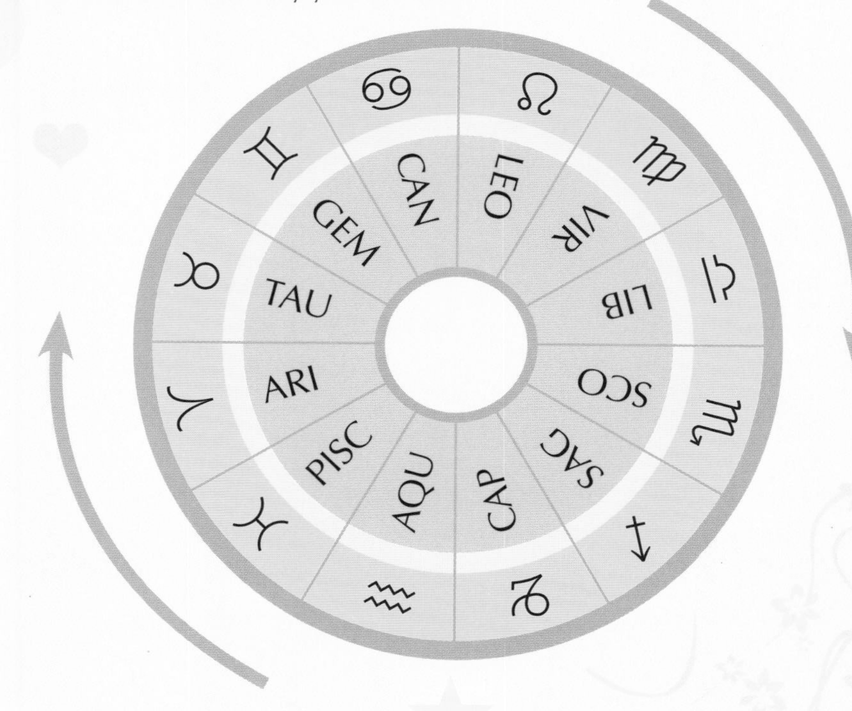

Aries Moon

The Lunar Ram

Ruled by headstrong Mars, yours is a take-charge Moon – and it shows, because you're no shrinking violet! You have a knack for spotting potential in situations and you spontaneously take the initiative. Bubbly and decisive, your natural inclination is to organize and to control.

As the Moon is associated with water (for example, the Moon rules the tides), it is not at its most comfortable in a Fire sign. At their best, fire and water produce steam and, as we all know, steam can drive an engine. At their worst, these elements work against each other – fire drying out water; water putting out fire.

Getting the best out of this Moon means learning to get the emotional balance right. Controlling the desire to take over every situation and every person you meet is the first step. Allowing others to meet you halfway and taking their views on board is the next. Having achieved that balance, you need to sustain the momentum.

Your fiery heart

Dynamic and independent, you're emotionally feisty and robust. You like to make your own decisions without consulting others and, until you learn to compromise, you may find it difficult to share.

That said, there is something noble about you and you seek the same emotional integrity in others. When it comes to settling down with a life-partner, you base your relationship on honesty and truth. Coupling up with someone as strong and independent as you is ideal, as this will challenge your fiery Moon. It will also help to diminish that sense of being tied down which makes you restless. When you do fall in love, you are a good partner who knows how to keep a relationship fresh.

EMOTIONAL KEYNOTES*: enthusiastic, romantic, hot, passionate, desirous, selfish, inconsiderate*

Aries Moon ...

... friend

People who get to know you soon discover what an open and straightforward friend you are. Cheerful and optimistic, you're a sociable character. You're drawn to people who are sporty and adventurous.

... parent

Domesticity may not be your strong suit, but when it comes to encouraging your children, you're right there! You'll train your kids to be independent from an early age, take them camping, teach them self-defence and cheer loudly for their team.

... in the workplace

You're full of bright ideas and keen to implement them. Ideally, work will keep you on the move, and let you call the shots, leading from the front. A stream of short-term projects will keep your interest.

... in love

You're deeply romantic and just plain sexy. In relationships you take the lead and may seem a little insensitive to more tender souls. As impulsive in love as you are in life, you're superb at the chat-up routine, but try not to come on too strong!

Lunar love chart

Your Aries Moon with their Moon or Sun in ...

◐◐◐◐	**ARIES** A pairing that's passionate and intense, you make good friends, but alas you're too competitive for long-lasting love.
◐◐	**TAURUS** Differing desires and lifestyles will drive the two of you apart.
◐◐◐◐	**GEMINI** Great! This interesting mixture can go far.
◐◐	**CANCER** A steamy pairing that needs a lot of work to succeed.
◐◐◐◐◐	**LEO** Wow! Hot, romantic, eager – this is such an exciting combination!
◐	**VIRGO** You two just aren't going to see eye-to-eye.
◐◐◐	**LIBRA** A possibility, if you're prepared to learn from each other.
◐◐◐	**SCORPIO** Your magnetic attraction makes you a dream team.
◐◐◐◐◐	**SAGITTARIUS** Athletic, adventurous, exciting – this is a scorcher of a partnership.
◐◐◐	**CAPRICORN** Better in the boardroom than the bedroom!
◐◐◐◐	**AQUARIUS** Plenty of mutual respect makes this a good, workable relationship.
◐◐	**PISCES** You'll be OK to begin with, but only a miracle will keep you together.

A GOOD MATCH?

◐ *prickly*

◐◐ *possible*

◐◐◐ *promising*

◐◐◐◐ *passionate*

◐◐◐◐◐ *perfect*

Taurus Moon

The Lunar Bull

Being responsible for moving the tides inevitably associates the Moon with water. As a sign, Taurus belongs to the Earth element, and Earth and Water are receptive to each other, together creating the fertile conditions in which plant life will grow. This mutually beneficial relationship means that, astrologically, the Moon is said to be "exalted" in the sign of Taurus – in other words, the Moon is comfortable here, imparting its finest characteristics.

Warm and loving, with your Moon in Taurus you build strong foundations in your life and create an atmosphere of beauty and peace around yourself and those you hold most dear. You are strongly attached to your family, and you like to keep them close, while your possessions give you a sense of permanence.

Your honest heart

In essence, a Taurean Moon stabilizes the moods, meaning that emotionally you are very together. Temperamentally constant, you're not prone to peaks of drama nor do you sink into troughs of despair. Whereas other people may go flakey in a crisis, throw a tantrum when they can't get their own way, or become downright hissy if asked to go the extra mile, not so with you. Born with great common sense, you don't go to pieces in an emergency. Nor do you play emotional games or turn your nose up at hard work. Instead, you roll up your sleeves and pitch in, invariably giving that ten-per-cent extra that makes you stand out as a thoroughly dependable and resourceful individual.

What's more, love-goddess Venus rules Taurus and imparts an essential sweetness to this sign. So, being born with the Moon in Taurus makes you especially blessed.

EMOTIONAL KEYNOTES*: charming, sensual, indulgent, sensible, relaxing, cautious, possessive*

Taurus Moon ...

... friend

Your charm and your outgoing smile draw people to you, and you love to make people feel at ease. Utterly trustworthy, you're always there for a friend in need.

... parent

No-one cossets their youngsters quite like you. You are one of the most protective parents around. You can be strict, though, and a little old-fashioned, insisting upon respect and good manners. Very artistic yourself, you enjoy watching your children blossom creatively.

... in the workplace

Whether you're the boss, a colleague or an employee, when you say you'll get a job done, you'll get it done. Dependable and down-to-earth, you handle tasks with common sense. You excel in creative occupations and love to work with Nature.

... in love

Being so emotionally steady and strong means that you're a rock to your partner. You're not impulsive or prone to mood swings, but you can be possessive. You take your time to fall in love but, once you commit, you're loyal to the end.

Lunar love chart

Your Taurus Moon with their Moon or Sun in …

◐◐	**ARIES** Doubtful. Realistically, you're just worlds apart.
◐◐◐◐	**TAURUS** You're a carbon copy of each other, making this partnership solid and secure.
◐	**GEMINI** A poor match. You have different mindsets and want different things in life.
◐◐◐◐	**CANCER** You're wonderfully cosy and comfortable.
◐◐◐	**LEO** You're well matched and you amuse each other, too.
◐◐◐◐◐	**VIRGO** A great combination! This partnership is solid, steady, supportive and lasting.
◐◐◐	**LIBRA** A sensual, creative and artistic couple.
◐◐◐	**SCORPIO** You may be opposites, but you're drawn together.
◐	**SAGITTARIUS** You pull apart in too many ways.
◐◐◐◐◐	**CAPRICORN** A powerful and enduring partnership – together, you're terrific!
◐◐	**AQUARIUS** A lack of trust divides you.
◐◐◐	**PISCES** Full of possibility – there's lots of mutual attraction here.

A GOOD MATCH?

◐ prickly

◐◐ possible

◐◐◐ promising

◐◐◐◐ passionate

◐◐◐◐◐ perfect

Gemini Moon

The Lunar Twins

A Gemini Moon is like champagne: light, bubbly, effervescent and it makes the party go with a swing. The Moon is associated with water, and Gemini is ruled by the element Air. Mixed together, these two make iridescent bubbles that sparkle and shimmer as they catch the light.

That analogy describes you so well! Outgoing and expressive, your chitter-chatter raises our spirits. No matter what company you're in, your wit sparkles as you pick up this conversation or that mood, keeping everyone entertained. But you can be easily distracted, flitting from one person to another, from one subject to the next.

Is it possible to have too much of a good thing? Unless you learn to focus, it is. Remember that too many bubbles can create a superficial sea of froth that is likely to blow away in the wind.

Your playful heart

Your Gemini Moon stimulates your curiosity, quickens your thought processes and endows you with both emotional shrewdness and linguistic ability. Communication is your forte and you don't shy away from expressing how you feel. And, blessed with a lively imagination, you can charm the birds out of the trees (and talk the hind leg off a donkey)!

You're as restless in relationships as you are in life, needing constant change, a multitude of interests and an address book full of friends. Boredom is your biggest enemy. Perhaps that's why you're always on the go, and you're forever on the lookout for the next person to amuse you. You're bright as a button and fun to be with, and this Moon keeps your emotions and spirit young at heart.

***EMOTIONAL KEYNOTES**: sparkling, witty, entertaining, lighthearted, intelligent, flirty, inconstant*

Gemini Moon ...

... friend

With your effortless ability to talk to anyone about anything, you make friends wherever you go. Amusing and lighthearted, you're at your best in a crowd. The more friends and acquaintances you have, the happier you are.

... parent

Because your Moon gives you the gift of youthfulness, being on the same wavelength as your children comes naturally to you. You never tire of playing games, telling stories or buying gadgets. Where you're concerned, there's no such thing as a generation gap.

... in the workplace

Bright, sharp and versatile, you love variety and pick up skills in a flash. You're happiest in a lively atmosphere, exchanging news and views with other people.

... in love

You're as prone to juggling admirers as you are to multi-tasking other areas of your life. You're sociable but you can be a flirt – even when in a couple. However, you're immensely witty and entertaining, and your partner loves you for it!

Your Gemini Moon with their Moon or Sun in ...

◐◐◐◐	**ARIES** High energy and activity keep your relationship evergreen.
◐	**TAURUS** You're both chatty, but are you talking the same language?
◐◐◐◐	**GEMINI** You're a pairing that is light, bubbly and fun.
◐◐	**CANCER** A clash of lifestyles makes this a difficult combination for a lasting union.
◐◐◐◐	**LEO** You make a sparkling couple.
◐◐◐	**VIRGO** Intellectually you're interesting, but romantically, sadly, you're a dull pair.
◐◐◐◐◐	**LIBRA** Great! You think alike and enjoy the same things.
◐	**SCORPIO** Alas, you're not a match made in heaven.
◐◐◐	**SAGITTARIUS** Fascinating – you're opposites, but that could work in your favour.
◐	**CAPRICORN** Sadly, the two of you are just not on the same emotional wavelength.
◐◐◐◐◐	**AQUARIUS** Your shared interests and aims in life make this a winning team.
◐◐	**PISCES** A confusing partnership, but you're potentially good companions.

A GOOD MATCH?

◐ prickly
◐◐ possible
◐◐◐ promising
◐◐◐◐ passionate
◐◐◐◐◐ perfect

Cancer Moon

The Lunar Crab

The Moon is Cancer's natural ruler, making it comfortably placed in this sign. In fact, the Moon is not only comfortable here, it's right at home. Both the Moon and Cancer are associated with the Water element, and both are synonymous with feelings and emotions. Being born under the Moon in Cancer, then, means that your emotional life is at the forefront of all you do.

You are also wonderfully sentimental. You treasure the past, and believe in conservation and preserving our heritage. Perhaps that's what makes you such a great collector. You're blessed with deep intuition and an excellent business sense.

And you have a formidable memory that serves you well – rarely do you forget an important birthday or special occasion.

Your loving heart

Born under a Cancer Moon, you're ruled by your feelings and, just as the Moon waxes and wanes, so your moods tend to fluctuate. Like the Crab that symbolizes this sign, you like to be tucked up safe and warm, and to protect your soft, tender feelings with a hard outer veneer. You can be sunshiny, scuttling about on the hot beach of life; but when your feelings are hurt, you crabbily withdraw inside your shell and refuse to budge until you sense that the coast is clear.

Hugely sensitive, you're a tender soul. You do get hurt easily by other people's insensitivity, but age and experience have taught you to mask your vulnerabilities well. Your heart is devoted to your home and family: you're happiest surrounded by your loved ones in your own house, or pottering around in your garden. You're one of life's carers – loving, considerate and kind.

EMOTIONAL KEYNOTES: *loving, caring, sensitive, nurturing, home-loving, defensive, moody*

Cancer Moon ...

... friend

Helpful, caring and sympathetic, you'll drop anything for a friend in need. You worry about your close friends, sometimes taking on their problems as your own. You're a good listener, appreciated for your discretion.

... parent

You're a storybook parent: all cosy home and bear hugs. You fuss over your children's well-being, teaching them family values and spoiling them with attention. But you believe in discipline, too, and expect your youngsters to be well behaved.

... in the workplace

Earning a good living is important to you, so your job has to pay well. Working from home puts you in seventh heaven, but you also like the security of being part of a larger, protective organization.

... in love

Yours is a tender heart that nurtures and protects. Despite your tough exterior, you're a sensitive soul and, emotionally, you bruise easily. But you're a born romantic, happy to cuddle up and make a home with the one you love.

Lunar love chart

Your Cancer Moon with their Moon or Sun in …

◐	**ARIES** This pairing is too fiery for your emotional sensibilities.
◐◐◐◐	**TAURUS** A partnership that simply goes on getting better and better.
◐	**GEMINI** Unlikely. Emotionally the two of you are at odds.
◐◐◐◐◐	**CANCER** Perfect! You're totally on the same plane.
◐◐◐	**LEO** A loving partnership, but exhausting.
◐◐◐◐	**VIRGO** A partnership that is mutually enriching.
◐	**LIBRA** Alas, a pairing with nowhere to go – the two of you are looking in opposite directions.
◐◐◐◐◐	**SCORPIO** A winning combination – there's plenty of deep respect, love and protection here.
◐◐	**SAGITTARIUS** A fidgety match – the two of you make for a restless relationship.
◐◐◐	**CAPRICORN** Although you're opposites, you're actually quite good for each other.
◐◐	**AQUARIUS** This pairing is too erratic to meet your need for emotional comfort.
◐◐◐◐◐	**PISCES** A deeply loving and caring match.

A GOOD MATCH?

◐ prickly
◐◐ possible
◐◐◐ promising
◐◐◐◐ passionate
◐◐◐◐◐ perfect

Leo Moon

The Lunar Lion

In Leo, the Moon is swathed in glamour. If you were born with the Moon in this sign, enjoyment and pleasure come before duty and obligation. You have big appetites and love the good things in life.

The Moon belongs to the Water element, while Leo, ruled by the Sun, is a fire sign. These two make a steamy mixture that is hot, passionate and volatile. Creativity, vitality, determination and taking control are all associated with the Leo Moon. Gorgeous, colourful and magnetic, you can't help but be an attention-seeker. Just as we all feel brighter, more joyous and more laid back when the Sun shines, so you feel happier, more positive and generally better about yourself when you're basking in the bright glow of the spotlight.

Your warming heart

Charismatic and spontaneously affectionate, you have a kind and generous heart. You're a bright, sparkling personality with a big smile and an infectious zest for life. A great organizer and a natural-born leader, you possess magnetic qualities, as well as dignity, pride and an aristocratic bearing that those around you can't help but want to know and love.

You have an irresistible appeal that others immediately warm to – which is lucky, as being loved is of paramount importance to you; and being popular, admired, praised and patted on the back are fundamental to your well-being. Like the Sun that rules your Moon sign, you need to feel that you're at the centre of things. Being ignored, forgotten or elbowed out of the way is like the Sun setting on your world and the dark of the night entering your soul.

EMOTIONAL KEYNOTES*: romantic, generous, loving, daring, playful, egotistical, over-the-top*

... friend

Generous and fun to be with, you're popular and well-liked. You're renowned for your kindness and are always ready to offer a helping hand.

... parent

You can't help but spoil your children. Standards and appearance are important to you, so you'll ensure they dress well, look their best and behave like angels. You fill their diaries with dancing, music and drama lessons, and you're always there in the audience to applaud – and secretly wipe away the tears of pride.

... in the workplace

All the world's your stage! To be fulfilled at work, you need recognition for your efforts. You're not happy in a lowly position, but you shine when given status. Ideally, though, you prefer to be the boss.

... in love

Your Moon is passionate and warm. Prone to the odd emotional drama, you are on the whole loving and giving, and truly happy in a close relationship. You are devoted to the one you love and tend to put your partner on a pedestal.

Your Leo Moon with their Moon or Sun in …

◐◐◐◐◐	**ARIES** There's a natural attraction in this partnership – and the sex is good, too!
◐◐	**TAURUS** A tricky combination – you're both inflexible and that doesn't bode so well.
◐◐◐◐	**GEMINI** Sparkling! This is a love match that's effervescent.
◐◐◐	**CANCER** The two of you are devoted and loyal.
◐◐◐◐◐	**LEO** Fabulous! You make a colourful pair enjoying the high life.
◐	**VIRGO** This pairing is unforgiving.
◐◐◐◐	**LIBRA** You two make the most affectionate union.
◐◐	**SCORPIO** Batten down the hatches – in this partnership stormy weather lies ahead!
◐◐◐◐◐	**SAGITTARIUS** With chemistry this good, you're made for each other.
◐	**CAPRICORN** Too dangerous for you – you're out of your comfort zone in this relationship.
◐◐◐	**AQUARIUS** Combine your efforts and together you'll have a great time.
◐◐	**PISCES** Soft, dreamy and romantic – but is it just altogether too good to last?

A GOOD MATCH?

◐ prickly

◐◐ possible

◐◐◐ promising

◐◐◐◐ passionate

◐◐◐◐◐ perfect

Virgo Moon

The Lunar Maiden

Mercury, the planet named after the god of medicine and well-being, rules your Moon sign, which is probably why you tend to concern yourself more than most with matters of health. Keeping fit, caring for others and ensuring that your family is fed a nutritious, balanced diet take priority in your scheme of things.

The Moon's association with the Water element means that it finds an affinity with Earthy signs such as Virgo. Earth needs water to create fertile conditions. But the balance has to be just right – too much water turns a field to mud; too little, and the soil remains barren. You, too, must strive to find the right physical, mental and emotional balance. Being off-kilter makes you feel unwell and can lead to obsessions and hang-ups. But when all is in harmony, being born with the Moon in Virgo ensures you'll live a happy, healthy life.

Your caring heart

Down-to-earth and hardworking, you're one of life's high achievers with standards that demand perfection. You love your family and are an honest, deeply caring provider, but you're also a worrier. You fret if things aren't just so and fuss over details that others wouldn't bat an eyelid about. You also worry about falling in love because you have a fundamental fear of being hurt.

An organizer par excellence, you're brilliant at creating order out of chaos. Intellectually sharp and emotionally astute, nothing escapes your attention. Your ability to study, your patience and your talent for investigation will take you far in life. And your caring approach, especially toward the ones you love, will bring you great respect and many devoted followers.

EMOTIONAL KEYNOTES*: shy, clever, discriminating, supportive, nature-loving, anxiety-prone, fastidious*

Virgo Moon ...

... friend

Although people may think you cold at first, once the ice has been broken, you warm to become a staunch ally, appreciated for your common sense. Clever and confident, with calm efficiency, you're a wonderful friend in a crisis.

... parent

You're a stickler for detail – clean hands, tidy bedroom. Hugely supportive, you're always there to help with homework and you encourage your children to continue their education, teaching them that success comes through hard work.

... in the workplace

Thorough and painstaking, few can match your organizational talents. Valued for your sharp eye for detail, you're well suited to occupations where critical judgment is of the essence.

... in love

Fundamentally shy and cautious, you don't readily fall in love. When you do, you take your relationships and your promises seriously. A laid-back partner who can make you laugh and relax is the ideal soulmate for you.

Your Virgo Moon with their Moon or Sun in ...

◐◐	**ARIES** Only if you want to live on the edge – this could be a dangerous liaison.
◐◐◐◐◐	**TAURUS** This loving relationship will bloom and blossom perfectly.
◐◐◐	**GEMINI** Intellectually you're OK together, but otherwise this sign's too flippant for you.
◐◐◐◐	**CANCER** A safe bet – this partnership is wonderfully settled.
◐	**LEO** This could be an emotional rollercoaster that proves uncomfortably dramatic.
◐◐◐◐◐	**VIRGO** In thinking, working and loving, you're like two peas in a pod.
◐	**LIBRA** A partnership that's too airy-fairy to last.
◐◐◐	**SCORPIO** Could be intriguing, but for how long?
◐	**SAGITTARIUS** Steer clear of this pairing – your worlds are simply poles apart.
◐◐◐◐◐	**CAPRICORN** Lovely – find your heart's ease here.
◐◐	**AQUARIUS** Ethical differences divide you.
◐◐◐	**PISCES** If you're both prepared to give and take, this pairing of opposites could lead to success.

A GOOD MATCH?

◐ prickly

◐◐ possible

◐◐◐ promising

◐◐◐◐ passionate

◐◐◐◐◐ perfect

Libra Moon

The Lunar Scales

You're fortunate indeed to have been born with the Moon in this sign. Like a precious stone that has been smoothed and buffed to a high shine, here the gentle and refined influences of Libra polish out any rough emotional edges.

Libra is affiliated to the Air group of elements, while the Moon is associated with Water. When air and water meet, they form a gentle, moist breeze that cools the hottest of days. Through your powers of diplomacy, you, too, have an ability to lower the temperature between people locked in heated or emotional arguments: you're a supreme negotiator, always ready to balance opposing points of view and to see the other side of the coin. Libra is ruled by Venus, who is the goddess not only of love, but also of luck and looks. Image is crucial for you, influencing both how you dress and present yourself, and your judgment of others. This Moon sign blesses you with grace and poise, with good manners and, in particular, with an abundance of charm.

Your friendly heart

Venus and the Moon are harmoniously disposed to one another, as each has an essential "femininity". This gives you your placid, receptive nature that makes you so amiable and relaxed.

Emotional stability is crucial to you. You thrive when you're settled, when you enjoy your work and when you're in tune with your partner and living in a pleasing environment. Uncongenial surroundings, arguments and mess disturb your sensibilities. An easy, pleasant, indulged life is what you seek and, with this lucky Moon, it's odds-on that's what you'll get.

EMOTIONAL KEYNOTES*: affable, charming, sociable, tactful, balanced, indecisive, evasive*

Libra Moon ...

... friend

You have terrific charm, so it's no wonder people find you easy to get along with. Intelligent and engaging, you're a delightful talker and a great listener. You're happiest among sophisticated people in congenial surroundings.

... parent

No matter how many children you have, you're even-handed. You expect your youngsters to be well-groomed, well-dressed and well-spoken. Administering discipline isn't easy for you, and often you'll walk away from an argument.

... in the workplace

Steer clear of messy environments and head instead for an upmarket office in a choice location. Colleagues will seek out your sense of fair play whenever a situation requires critical judgment.

... in love

You're never happier than when you're in a one-to-one – but it takes a while for you to make up your mind on whom to commit to! Looks are important to you, so you'll fall for someone who's good-looking and well-dressed.

Lunar love chart

Your Libra Moon with their Moon or Sun in …

◐◐◐	**ARIES** Tricky, but worth a go – this partner complements you well.
◐◐◐	**TAURUS** Together, you can enjoy the finer things in life.
◐◐◐◐◐	**GEMINI** Animal attraction! Instinctively, the two of you are drawn to each other.
◐	**CANCER** Too wobbly! This relationship will disturb your carefully guarded sense of equilibrium.
◐◐◐◐	**LEO** Lovely! You have plenty of complementary interests to share with each other.
◐◐	**VIRGO** Alas, no. This one's too fussy for words!
◐◐◐◐◐	**LIBRA** You're happy in each other's company and well-suited, too.
◐◐◐	**SCORPIO** This could be tough – beware a battle of wills.
◐◐◐◐	**SAGITTARIUS** A most agreeable and enjoyable togetherness.
◐	**CAPRICORN** This partnership is great for business, but perhaps not so great for love.
◐◐◐◐◐	**AQUARIUS** A meeting of hearts and minds.
◐◐◐	**PISCES** Sensitive, creative and romantic – you're so attuned!

A GOOD MATCH?

◐ prickly

◐◐ possible

◐◐◐ promising

◐◐◐◐ passionate

◐◐◐◐◐ perfect

Scorpio Moon

The Lunar Scorpion

Yours is a powerful Moon – deep, dark and driven. Scorpio is an intensely secretive and private sign. The Moon is moody and changeable; sometimes high, sometimes low. When combined, these two produce a brooding presence.

Both the Moon and Scorpio are associated with the Water element. With this combination, your feelings demand superhuman control. Thoughts, memories and emotions rush at you like a thunderstorm, a deluge with currents that sweep you away. Here, there is desire and, like a river that never stops flowing, a constant search for the answer that will satisfy what you're looking for.

A natural-born psychologist, you have a clever knack of seeing straight through people and situations. It means that you know how to pull all the right strings and press all the right buttons. Ruled by Pluto, the planet of regeneration, you are like the phoenix who can rise from the ashes and recreate yourself at will.

Your passionate heart

There's something magnetically attractive about you – you ooze sexuality. But there's also mystery, which makes you prone to introspection. A private person, you take yourself and your life seriously. Emotions are either black or white for you and rarely are they relaxed or comfortable. One minute your feelings will tend to hit the heights of elation and the next they will plunge to the depths of despair. To those you know and love, you give total loyalty – and you demand the same commitment from them in return. You may be prone to jealousy and you never forget a betrayal.

EMOTIONAL KEYNOTES*: passionate, totally committed, loyal, exclusive, intense, jealous, brooding*

Scorpio Moon ...

... friend

People are attracted by your clever, satirical manner. But you don't suffer fools gladly and are selective about your friends. You live by loyalty and respect.

... parent

Totally devoted to your family, you can be overprotective. You love your youngsters with a passion, but you expect obedience and respect. Allowing your children greater freedom to experiment and explore life will ease potential battles of will in their teenage years.

... in the workplace

If there's a need to get to the bottom of a mystery, there you'll be. Your single-mindedness means that once you have the bit between your teeth, you rarely let go. With steady hand–eye co-ordination, you excel in handling precision tools.

... in love

Members of the opposite sex are magnetically drawn to your charms. Your need for secrecy adds to your mystique and augments your strong sex drive. In love, it's all-or-nothing and once you've pledged your affection, it's for life.

Lunar love chart

Your Scorpio Moon with their Moon or Sun in ...

◐◐◐◐	**ARIES** This can be a rewarding relationship despite the emotional dramas.
◐◐◐	**TAURUS** You may be opposites, but you have what it takes to make this relationship work!
◐	**GEMINI** A difficult love match.
◐◐◐◐◐	**CANCER** Wonderful! You respond intuitively to each other.
◐◐◐	**LEO** In this partnership sparks will fly – negatively as well as positively.
◐◐◐	**VIRGO** A relationship that's mutually supportive despite your ever-fluctuating desires.
◐◐	**LIBRA** This pairing makes for an on–off affair.
◐◐◐◐◐	**SCORPIO** Together you're strong, potent, dynamic, intense and quite simply ... wonderful!
◐◐	**SAGITTARIUS** At best, this is a volatile union.
◐◐◐◐	**CAPRICORN** A satisfying romantic liaison.
◐◐◐	**AQUARIUS** This partnership will prove companionable but unsettling.
◐◐◐◐◐	**PISCES** Perfect! The two of you will form intense and lasting bonds.

A GOOD MATCH?

◐ prickly

◐◐ possible

◐◐◐ promising

◐◐◐◐ passionate

◐◐◐◐◐ perfect

Sagittarius Moon

The Lunar Archer

Fire and Water are mixed in copious quantities in your Moon sign. Together, these two generate great clouds of hot steam that float ever skyward. And just like those clouds, the Sagittarius Moon is constantly moving, searching for whatever is just out of reach or around the next corner.

Big-hearted, jovial Jupiter is the ruler of your Moon, blessing you with an easygoing disposition and a desire to live life to the full. As "think bigger" and "the more the merrier" are Jupiter's slogans, it's a natural consequence that you've been given such a vast appetite: you take on far more than you can handle, you push yourself to the limit and you burn the candle at both ends. Strangely, and against all expectations, you seem to beat the odds and succeed where lesser mortals would fail.

Your soaring heart

Life is far too short to waste time on detail! With your love of roaming and reading, you shun the ties that hamper or hinder your liberty. For you, the world is full of excitement, challenges and temptations. As long as there's variety and adventure in your life, fresh experiences to enjoy every day and distant horizons that beckon – intellectually and emotionally as well as physically – your spirit is ecstatic.

Relaxed and friendly, you're an affable soul to have around. You like company, but you value your own space highly, and never want to be emotionally hemmed in. With your positivity, good fortune always knocks at your door.

EMOTIONAL KEYNOTES*: easygoing, enthusiastic, friendly, philosophical, understanding, restless, tactless*

Sagittarius Moon ...

... friend

People can't fail but respond to your disarmingly open smile! You have a natural gift for brightening up even the dullest of days. You always have an amusing story to tell, and you bring instant cheer to whoever you're with.

... parent

Being so genial, tolerant and fun-loving makes you an easygoing parent. You're passionate about education and turn most activities into learning situations. Relaxed and informal, you abhor strict routines.

... in the workplace

Philosophical and far-sighted, you excel in occupations that allow you to see the bigger picture, but invariably you take on more than you should. You're a natural instructor, speaker and demonstrator.

... in love

It's your happy-go-lucky manner that makes you so attractive. As a companion, you're playful and affectionate, but being tied down makes you restless. You need a clever partner who will acknowledge your need for personal space.

Lunar love chart

Your Sagittarius Moon with their Moon or Sun in ...

◐◐◐◐◐	**ARIES** A partnership with lots of wonderful warmth and enthusiasm to share.
◐	**TAURUS** Neither of you will want to change to accommodate the other's needs and desires.
◐◐◐	**GEMINI** Surprisingly, you have more in common than at first appears.
◐◐	**CANCER** These love ties can hem you in.
◐◐◐◐◐	**LEO** Perfect! A true love match in every sense.
◐	**VIRGO** Your ardent nature finds this partner far too cool for a successful relationship.
◐◐◐◐	**LIBRA** You two make an interesting recipe for romance.
◐◐	**SCORPIO** This partner's intense moods will wear you down.
◐◐◐◐◐	**SAGITTARIUS** A deep and instinctive understanding unites you.
◐	**CAPRICORN** Far too distant. Your inner needs are poles apart.
◐◐◐◐	**AQUARIUS** You appreciate each other so much.
◐◐◐	**PISCES** Spiritually, the two of you are ideal, but practically, you're mismatched.

A GOOD MATCH?

◐ prickly

◐◐ possible

◐◐◐ promising

◐◐◐◐ passionate

◐◐◐◐◐ perfect

Capricorn Moon

The Lunar Mountain Goat

Capricorn belongs to the Earth element – grounded and practical. Although the Moon is associated with Water, which should provide moisture to engender plant life, here Earth is not so much the fertile garden of Taurus, nor the friable soil of Virgo; it is the bedrock upon which we lay our very foundations.

Yours is one of the most industrious and, arguably, the most ambitious of all the Moon signs. Position and wealth are what you aspire to, and you work diligently to reach your goal. It may take a lifetime but, as you are ruled by Saturn, the Father of Time, you have patience on your side. Slowly, through sheer hard work, you build

your reputation, and you invest your money knowing that one day, like the sure-footed mountain goat that represents your Moon sign, you will reach the top.

Your dependable heart

Emotionally solid and robust, for you life is a serious business. With Saturn, ruler of discipline and structure, governing your Moon sign, it's natural for you to put duty and responsibility before your own pleasure and happiness. Like all Earth signs, you're primarily logical. Your head rules your heart – every time!

There is a danger on first meeting new people that you may come across as emotionally detached – to strangers, you can appear emotionally over-cautious. However, as they get to know you, people discover what a delicious sense of humour you have, as well as how witty and wry you can be. Mature beyond your years, you're reliable, sophisticated and wise.

EMOTIONAL KEYNOTES*: supportive, responsible, good provider, mature, sensible, reserved, detached*

Capricorn Moon ...

... friend

To those who get to know you, you're a loyal friend – someone capable of giving true and genuine affection. Being a good listener makes you popular, and that dry sense of humour of yours is just a sheer delight.

... parent

You're a great believer in rules, which makes you a super-efficient parent in a household that runs like clockwork. You swell with pride when your children work hard to succeed and better themselves.

... in the workplace

Mature and responsible, you take your duties seriously and work long hours. Fiercely ambitious, your drive to excel can turn you into a workaholic.

... in love

Practical and sensible, you don't have time for sentimentality or silly emotional games. Instead, you take a robust approach to love, but because of this you may come across as cool and aloof. Hitching up with someone who is both a business and an intimate partner is your ideal.

Lunar love chart

Your Capricorn Moon with their Moon or Sun in …

◐◐◐	**ARIES** This makes a gritty combination, but it's worth a go!
◐◐◐◐◐	**TAURUS** Deep love, appreciation and respect can flourish here.
◐	**GEMINI** Too changeable. This relationship makes you feel far too insecure.
◐◐◐	**CANCER** You may be opposites, but together you can enjoy growing rich.
◐◐◐	**LEO** Challenging – but in the right circumstances you could be good for each other.
◐◐◐◐◐	**VIRGO** This affair of the heart is just meant to be!
◐	**LIBRA** Disagreements will drive you apart.
◐◐◐◐	**SCORPIO** Struck by lightning? This is an utterly spontaneous attraction – it's love at first sight!
◐	**SAGITTARIUS** Only with a great deal of effort and understanding will this relationship work.
◐◐◐◐◐	**CAPRICORN** Together, you two will achieve so much!
◐◐◐	**AQUARIUS** You're philosophically at odds.
◐◐◐	**PISCES** There's a lot of comfort here to give and to share.

A GOOD MATCH?

◐ prickly
◐◐ possible
◐◐◐ promising
◐◐◐◐ passionate
◐◐◐◐◐ perfect

Aquarius Moon

The Lunar Water Carrier

Despite the water jug that symbolizes your Moon sign, Aquarius is ruled by the element Air. All Air signs are associated with the intellect. The Moon, aside from governing the emotions and moods, rules the imagination, probing deep into our thought processes and connecting the mind with the collective unconscious. Your Aquarius Moon gives you the vision to cut through the pretensions and red tape that hinder the flowering of new ideas.

This is a zany Moon. In this sign, Air and Water mix like the frothy head on a pint of beer that tickles your nose as you sip. The Aquarius Moon is unconventional, a surprise-a-minute, an acquired taste. It's an unexpectedly heady brew, that eases tension yet also stimulates the senses.

Your courageous heart

In Aquarius, the Moon is in fertile creative territory – original, far-seeing and future-oriented. Being so far ahead with your thinking can make you seem emotionally erratic, but your ability to solve problems can at times earn you the status of genius. And anyway, you can't help being different.

In relationships, age discrepancies don't faze you. You may also make unusual choices regarding differences in gender, culture, creed, colour, shape or size – if anyone can make an unexpected, surprising and unconventional relationship work, you can. Spontaneous, original and inventive, you're never afraid to experiment and to break new ground. Controversial you may be, but you're also tolerant and broad-minded toward others – altogether a very welcome breath of fresh air.

***EMOTIONAL KEYNOTES**: friendly, sincere, original, experimental, tolerant, distant, eccentric*

Aquarius Moon ...

... friend

Friendly and sociable, you're never happier than when surrounded by like minds; your friends are like family to you. You're sometimes reflective and sometimes the life-and-soul – it's just part of your unpredictable nature.

... parent

Experimental, unorthodox and laid-back sum up your ideas about child-rearing. You encourage your children to explore their world and to think for themselves. Although you're fairly lax over discipline, you do insist upon complete honesty.

... in the workplace

Whatever your occupation, if there's room for innovation, you'll find it. You're inventive, will try anything new and can see beyond the present, so you're always way ahead of the game.

... in love

Just because you're not cuddly doesn't mean you're not loving. For you, love is an intellectual expression based on mutual trust and interests. You don't suffer pangs of jealousy – in fact, a free-and-easy relationship is your ideal.

Lunar love chart

Your Aquarius Moon with their Moon or Sun in ...

◐◐◐	**ARIES** A partnership that's independent, adventurous and interesting.
◐	**TAURUS** Lacks zing! Too stolid for you by far.
◐◐◐◐◐	**GEMINI** A tantalizing affair that could last a lifetime.
◐	**CANCER** Frankly, you might find this relationship just a little boring.
◐◐◐	**LEO** You may be opposites, but this union could really sizzle!
◐◐	**VIRGO** You are well matched intellectually, but your worldly ambitions are poles apart.
◐◐◐◐◐	**LIBRA** A love match that's so elegant, sophisticated and urbane.
◐◐◐	**SCORPIO** Take care – this partner's jealousy will inevitably clip your wings.
◐◐◐◐	**SAGITTARIUS** Interesting! This pairing provides a fascinating meeting of minds.
◐◐	**CAPRICORN** You'll have to agree to disagree if you want to make this relationship work.
◐◐◐◐◐	**AQUARIUS** Ideal. This partnership is inventive, intelligent and easy all the way.
◐◐◐	**PISCES** You meet each other on a higher level of understanding.

A GOOD MATCH?

◐ prickly

◐◐ possible

◐◐◐ promising

◐◐◐◐ passionate

◐◐◐◐◐ perfect

Pisces Moon

The Lunar Water Carrier

Water is your emotional element – from placid lake through sparkling waterfall to raging sea, your feelings move and change, washing over you like gigantic waves. Because you're sensitive, you're ever mindful of other people's feelings. This is a feminine, mutable Moon sign, which means that you're happy to flow with the changing tide. You're a mystically minded soul, who loves a peaceful, serene life.

Being born with the Moon in Pisces means that you're tender-hearted. No matter what image you present to the world, deep down you're sensitive, caring and compassionate. It's this spontaneous empathy that makes you a natural therapist, drawing you to the healing professions. You're great at listening to problems and you counsel with infinite understanding. Others find you so soothing and calming – everyone just feels better when you're there.

Your idealistic heart

Your Moon Sign is represented by a pair of fish tied together yet swimming in opposite directions. This imagery conveys your contradictory emotions, which make you laugh one minute and cry the next. You're frequently torn between fantasy and reality, love and duty, heaven and hell. And in the same way that the fish are bound to each other, you, too, strive for deep connection – and your ultimate desire is to achieve a truly perfect union through love.

You're the world's greatest romantic, and when you're in love, the sun shines brightly in your soul. Loving, affectionate and loyal, once you're settled, you're able to keep the magic alive.

EMOTIONAL KEYNOTES*: sensitive, compassionate, dreamy, imaginative, inspirational, romantic idealist, desires to please*

Pisces Moon …

… friend

Friendships run deep, and you quickly forge strong bonds with those you like. But be careful – you have a tendency to be too kind-hearted, and people may take advantage of your generosity and good nature.

… parent

You're a child at heart, and creating a magical wonderland for your children is sheer joy. You adore role-play and fantasy, dressing up and make-believe, but you prefer to leave discipline to others, because discord and disharmony upset you deeply.

… in the workplace

Creativity may be your niche, but your compassion lends itself to medical or caring professions. Colleagues like your loyalty; as a boss, you put the emotional needs of your workforce first. You crack the whip subtly, by appealing to people's feelings.

… in love

You're a bit of a fantasist, wanting the perfect romance – a superhuman who has no faults, no blemishes and no flaws. Do they exist? You like to think so, but it may take a while to find "the one".

Lunar love chart

Your Pisces Moon with their Moon or Sun in ...

◐◐	**ARIES** Emotionally the two of you are worlds apart – the agony and the ecstasy perhaps?
◐◐◐	**TAURUS** Your open hearts complement each other beautifully.
◐◐	**GEMINI** You're emotionally sensitive, and this sign can be too self-sufficient – it doesn't look good.
◐◐◐◐◐	**CANCER** Two hearts that are delightfully tender and true promise an ideal match.
◐◐	**LEO** You're a couple of romantics – could you share similar dreams?
◐◐◐	**VIRGO** You'll make good companions and good friends.
◐◐◐	**LIBRA** You're both looking for love – perhaps you could find it here?
◐◐◐◐◐	**SCORPIO** Your magnetic attraction makes you a dream team.
◐	**SAGITTARIUS** Deep divisions create resentments – a difficult match.
◐◐◐◐	**CAPRICORN** You're so good for each other.
◐◐◐	**AQUARIUS** It may not be trouble-free, but mutual fascination can cement this union.
◐◐◐◐◐	**PISCES** A dreamy, idealistic and blissful romance.

A GOOD MATCH?

◐ prickly

◐◐ possible

◐◐◐ promising

◐◐◐◐ passionate

◐◐◐◐◐ perfect

Timing for Success

The lunar cycle divides each month into two two-week periods, or fortnights. The first fortnight begins with a New Moon (the first lunation), while the second starts with a Full Moon (the second lunation). From New to Full is the waxing phase, when energies increase, growth is triggered and new developments begin. From Full back to New is the waning period. During this fortnight our energies lessen, we tire more easily, and we turn inward to become more introspective.

Most calendars carry the symbols for the two lunations so that you can check when they are due. A black disk (●) represents the New Moon and, two weeks later, a white circle (○) symbolizes the Full Moon.

The two lunar phases lend themselves to different activities. Identifying the fortnights and synchronizing with them enables us to tap into these subtle, yet powerful, natural forces. For example, start a new endeavour during the waxing fortnight, when we're eager to get on with things, and the project will fly along. Start it during the second fortnight, when impetus is lacking, and the job will just take longer to accomplish.

Working with the Moon: ***Use this table to synchronize your activities with the waxing and waning of the moon***

ACTIVITIES FOR THE WAXING FORTNIGHT (*from New Moon to Full Moon*)	ACTIVITIES FOR THE WANING FORTNIGHT (*from Full Moon to New Moon*)
Perform accruing, growing or lively activities during the waxing fortnight.	*Perform shedding, cutting or restful activities during the waning fortnight.*
◑ begin new projects ◑ sign contracts and agreements ◑ have your hair cut – it'll regrow faster if you hate the style ◑ get medical treatment ◑ put forward new ideas ◑ apply for a new job ◑ start construction work ◑ become engaged/get married ◑ start a new savings scheme ◑ plant flowers and vegetables ◑ interview job applicants ◑ advertise ◑ play sports ◑ redecorate ◑ throw a party	◐ go on a diet ◐ clear away clutter and rubbish ◐ have your hair cut – it'll be slow to grow, maintaining the style ◐ pluck your eyebrows ◐ prune trees ◐ mow the lawn ◐ carry out research ◐ settle disputes with loved ones ◐ relay bad news ◐ get separated or divorced ◐ bottle jams and pickles – they won't spoil ◐ arrange an intimate dinner with your partner ◐ make plans ◐ rest more

Making the Most of the Lunar Trends

The Sun takes a year to travel around the Zodiac, but the Moon zips through all twelve signs in a month, spending just two-and-a-quarter days in each! As the Moon moves in and out of each sign, it "picks up" influences and triggers in us different moods and responses. Using the charts on pages 72–5, discover which sign the Moon is in on any particular day – and understand how it is influencing you. With this information, you can swim with the lunar tide, rather than against it.

When the Moon is in ...

ARIES Apply for a job; join a sports club; have your hair restyled; visit the optician; buy metal objects and instruments.
buy: *sunglasses, hats, knives, a car* ***wear:*** *red*

TAURUS Check bank statements; start a new creative project; plant a tree; have a massage; arrange flowers; relax; pamper yourself.
buy: *scarves, perfume, seeds, music, chocolate, cakes* ***wear:*** *light blue*

GEMINI Call your friends; arrange a meeting; catch up on belated correspondence; write a story; learn something new; visit a sibling; make friends with your neighbours; sign a business contract.
buy: *stationery, magazines, a new book, maps, season tickets* ***wear:*** *yellow*

CANCER Visit your mother; clean the house; cook a special meal; read a history book; sow seeds; research your ancestry.
buy: *antique furniture, tickets for a cruise, food stocks* ***wear:*** *white*

LEO Go to the movies; visit an art gallery; ask a special someone out on a date; spend time practising your favourite hobby; watch a DVD; join your local amateur dramatics group.
buy: *tickets, mirrors, jewellery, presents, children's toys* ***wear:*** *flame orange*

VIRGO Make a doctor's appointment; groom your pets; file your papers; re-organize your schedule; revamp the kitchen; spring clean the house.
buy: *groceries, kitchen products, first-aid kit, toiletries* ***wear:*** *terracotta brown*

LIBRA Propose to your partner; get married; forge agreements; take on a business partner; make up a quarrel; merge with a company.
buy: *an engagement ring, a wedding dress, flowers* ***wear:*** *pastel pink*

SCORPIO De-clutter your house; join a search for buried treasure; read a detective novel; begin renovating a property; pay your taxes; check your insurance policies; seek information.
buy: *lingerie, an annuity, a cult horror film on DVD* ***wear:*** *black*

SAGITTARIUS Plan a holiday; enrol at college or university; go to a conference; contact people far away; engage a lawyer; take a long walk; visit a cathedral.
buy: *an atlas, sports gear, religious mementoes, travel guide book* ***wear:*** *purple*

CAPRICORN Update your CV/résumé); meet with the boss; apply for a promotion; mix business with pleasure; go out with influential friends; run in an election.
buy: *a business suit, a designer watch, a political memoir* ***wear:*** *navy*

AQUARIUS Meet with friends; ride in a hot-air balloon; review your aims; have your birth chart drawn up; meet with consultants; work for local government.
buy: *computers, hi-tech equipment, domestic appliances* ***wear:*** *electric blue*

PISCES Have a foot treatment; book a retreat; visit people in hospital; volunteer your services; meditate; donate to charity; take a "duvet" day; go to bed early.
buy: *socks, shoes, boots, alcoholic beverages* ***wear:*** *sea green*